AUTHORED BY

RAISING A SUCCESSFUL CHILD
(THE MANUAL)

PREFACE BY JOAN FRANKLIN SMUTNY

ISBN: 1456557912
ISBN-13: 9781456557911
LCCN: 2011901024

Brilliant in its simplicity in getting to the heart of what every parent needs to know To have a warm, loving relationship with their baby and raise a happy, healthy, Secure child. Author, teacher and nationally and internationally acclaimed lecturer, Dr. Mark McKee brings over thirty years of dedication and experience treating Children adolescents and their families, to this highly uplifting and important book. Dr. McKee helps parents navigate and decode what their baby really needs to thrive and challenges them to assess the "ghosts" in their nursery, so that they do not repeat unhealthy parenting practices learned from their past. Raising A Successful Child-the Manual beautifully lays the groundwork for everything that is vital to the parent child relationship. A "must read" for any parent and an absolute necessity for parents of newborns.

Elizabeth M. Frick, Psy.D.

Former Assistant Professor of Clinical Psychiatry, Northwestern University Medical School; Former Lecturer in Psychiatry, Stritch School of Medicine, Loyola University. Private Practice, Boston, Massachusetts

"The Manual" is a great, practical approach to help raise your child. Will recommend that all my patients' parents have it at their bedside, in the kitchen, in the car, and wherever they might need helpful hints as to how to handle tough situations.

James Pollack, MD
Pediatrician

Based on past successful parenting practices, and even more excitingly on fairly recent research findings that point to new directions in parenting, this book provides in clear and simple language, the tools for raising successful children. Dr. McKee has organized the complex activity of parenting into a manageable, step by step instructional guide which gives the developmental context in which each step takes place. He does not overwhelm the reader with too much information, but rather cites major parenting observations and research findings in a succinct and helpful manner. Parents who read this guide will find ways of looking at the particular challenges of raising a child with a

broader understanding as well as thoughtful ways to be with their child.

Marc Lubin, Ph.D.
Full Professor in Clinical Psychology
Argosy University/Orange County

In his book, *Raising A Successful Child*,
Dr. M. Mark McKee utilizes current research
in infant mental health and child development, as well as over 30 years of clinical
experience to provide parents with tools to
raising a self-sufficient and well adjusted
child. Written in a concise and practical
manner, Dr. McKee's manual provides a road
map to guide and direct parents in providing a positive foundation from which their
child can develop into a healthy and successful adult. *Raising A Successful Child* is
based on what parents *should* be doing, rather
than those things they should avoid and provides parents with valuable tips to building
a positive, playful, and mutually satisfying relationship with their child. Dr. McKee
also provides a wealth of information regard-
ing effective discipline practices and high-
lights parents' role in helping their child to

develop self-control and internal management abilities. This written manual is reflective of the professionalism, breadth of knowledge, and nurturance that Dr. McKee provides the patients within his own clinical practice.

Jennifer Duff, Psy.D.
Licensed Clinical Child Psychologist

Raising a Successful Child (The Manual) is a book that is long overdue. Dr. McKee has combined his years of experience with the latest information on child development to provide an easy to read and thoughtful guide to raising children. The Manual looks closely at the relationship between parents and children and is a positive guide to successful child rearing.In addition, the format of the book allows quick access and successful interventions to most questions parents face when raising and guiding children to become successful adults.

Joseph M. Nemeth, MD
Board Certified
Child and Adolescent Psychiatrist

In the last few years we have read and learned about the ill effects of "Helicopter Parents" (over) protecting their child's self-esteem. Just recently, we have been introduced to the idea of "tough parenting" as advocated by Tiger Mom Amy Chua. As always, the pendulum swings from one extreme to the other, while the real answers and healthy approaches to successful parenting reside in the healthy valley between over-indulgent and tough parenting. That is why every parent should read the no-nonsense straightforward parenting manual "Raising a Successful Child" by Dr. M.Mark McKee. This brilliant parenting book introduces parents to the idea of a balanced life for a child— work and play are equally important at all stages of development. Underlying his strong conviction for a balanced life, Dr. McKee's book is an easy-to —follow road map to help both child and parent develop a healthy, lov- ing, and, yes , successful life. For parents who are looking for answers amidst the clut- ter of extremes, "Raising a Successful Child (The Manual)" is a must-read book.

Ben Hebebrand
Head of School
Quest Academy
Palatine,Illinois

DEDICATION

To Jessica Shay and Austin Cole

TABLE OF CONTENTS

PREFACE

By Joan Franklin Smutny

There is no shortage of books on raising children. Yet, parents I know often find them too lengthy or fear-based to address their immediate concerns. Exploring all the things that can go wrong and what families should do to avoid these problems does little to build confidence in parents or children. Mark McKee's *Raising a Successful Child (The Manual)* departs from this trend, offering parents a concise, clearly written guide on the art of parenting that distills not only the most pertinent research on the subject but his own experience as a psychologist who has worked closely with families for over 20 years.

Centering his book around the theme of building a strong and healthy parent-child relationship, McKee offers parents a clear, accessible guide—no easy feat in a time when families face a dizzying array of advice from every side. His book tempers the hubbub of so many prescriptions and "how-to's" and gently guides parents to the most essential ingredient—the relationship they've been creating with their children from the first days of life. What parents discover, through this book, is that shifting attention from what their children are doing (or not doing) to the relationship will enable them to approach their challenges in a new way. The book inspires different sorts of questions than we commonly see in parenting books. Rather than, "How can I make my child perform better in school?" Or "How can I stop her tantrums whenever we go out?", new questions arise: "How can I build a relationship with my child that nurtures healthy growth and well-being for both of us? What would that look like? What does my child need from our relationship right now and what might I do differently?"

Unlike other published writing I've seen, this book looks deeply at the ecology of the parent-child relationship—that is, the specific ways it needs to respond to the natural changes in a child's cognitive, emotional, and social growth. What McKee shows is that when parents attend more to growing a strong and healthy relationship, when they carefully consider what they are bringing to it and then use the book's principles to nurture and sustain it, they will find the solutions they seek to a variety of problems. In the process, parents often become more proactive, more able to recognize new growth in their children and respond in appropriate ways. They begin to anticipate needs, rather than being caught off guard by behaviors they don't understand and then reacting in ways that don't work for their children.

Raising a Successful Child (The Manual) makes it clear that the most urgent demand upon parents is to *be with* their children. In practical terms, this means not merely sitting in the same room, but actually inter-acting in a way that builds and strengthens the relationship—playing, telling stories, sharing thoughts, going for walks, reading, making things, singing songs, and so forth. McKee offers many suggestions for making the time parents spend more beneficial in build-ing trust, stimulating curiosity, providing needed structure, and instilling the con-fidence that will enable their children to become more independent. Essential to this process, according to the author, is self-awareness on the part of parents with regard to their own inherited ideas about child-rearing. Equipped with the information in this book, parents can weigh the assumptions they've acquired from their own family his-tory, social networks, and the media against the facts, and thereby develop more informed responses to the particular needs or struggles of their own children.

Since *The Manual* presents a relationship-based approach to parenting, it makes sense that the question of discipline should come at the end. Though important, discipline works best in the context of a strong, mutually beneficial parent-child relationship. McKee provides sensitive, perceptive guidelines for parents on how to structure their children's experiences in ways that promote growth in confidence and self-control. He illustrates in concrete ways how parents can help children understand the idea of consequences so that they can connect their own behaviors to the circumstances that follow. *Raising a Successful Child (The Manual)* presents discipline as another dimension of parents relating to their children where the possibility of becoming self-disciplined comes with practice, patient reinforcement, and sometimes, the smallest of steps.

Raising a Successful Child (The Manual) is an eminently humane book, by which I mean that it steers clear of alarmist sentiments or vignettes of struggling parents, and instead guides readers to an essential wisdom on tending the parent-child relationship. This may sound simple, but it is a profound undertaking. Any parent who reads this manual will assuredly re-visit its pages again and again, and will find in its wise counsel the most trustworthy and sustaining support for raising their children.

ACKNOWLEDGMENTS

As with all books, this book is the result of the input and support of many. The children and parents I have seen over the past thirty years who allowed me to enter their worlds has been an honor. My intellectual and academic mentors-and at times my emotional guides-helped me develop capacities for observing, understanding and intervening that has served and continues to serve as the foundation for my professional (and at times personal) life. I would especially like to acknowledge Dr. Garry Landreth, Dr. Marc Lubin and Dr. Robert Langs in this regard.

I would like to express my profound appreciation to Dr. Marc Lubin, Dr. Elizabeth Frick, Dr. Jennifer Duff, Dr. Joe Nemeth, Ben Hebebrand, and Dr. James Pollack for extending their time and energy to review my work. Joan Smutny's support for my work with children over the past many years as well as her gracious encouragement of my work has been a gift.

I am forever grateful to my mother for introducing me to books and her encouragement to pursue dreams; my father for teaching me how to work so that dreams have become reality and to my sister for her constant model of perseverance=achievement . Further, there is simply no way this book would exist without the love, support and capacity to allow me the space and time to complete my work that my wife, Daphne, has always freely given.

Finally , Norma McKittrick's editorial work was invaluable as she transformed my academic and professional writing into a readable format. In addition, the staff at createspace has been an absolute pleasure to work with throughout the entire process from submission of my idea to the completion of this book.

INTRODUCTION

If you want to raise a child who will grow up to become a successful, self-sufficient, well-adjusted adult, you must commit to making an ongoing investment of yourself in the life of that child. You must be willing to freely spend your time, energy, and love in developing a positive relationship with your child, a relationship that will provide the support, encouragement, and guidance your child requires at the various stages of his/her physical, mental, and emotional development. *Raising a Successful Child (The Manual)* will give you the core knowledge you need to understand what your child requires at each stage of his/her development and how you can best meet those needs.

I have written *Raising a Successful Child (The Manual)* in response to numerous requests for information that would help adults develop a road map for raising their children. The parents I have met over the past thirty-five years have asked for a concise book that addresses the positive issues and tells what to do, rather than what to avoid. Parents also want to know about the emotional and social aspects of parent-child relationships and how to establish and maintain healthy relationships with their children.

Many parents joke that they were not issued a manual for raising a child. Thus, this book serves as the first manual parents need.

While this book bypasses some issues related to the physical development and caretaking of children (primarily because that information is readily available from other sources), it still provides the "big picture" of parenting. In addition it provides very specific information about what parents must do to develop positive, adaptive, pleasurable relationships that enhance their child's healthy, emotional development.

Parents asked me for a book that gives research-supported information rather than personalized vignettes or emotionally told stories and case studies. Thus I have based *Raising a Successful Child (The Manual)* on recent findings about infant mental health and child development. In the past twenty years some exciting studies have pointed to new directions in parenting, while other studies have clearly indicated that those parenting practices that have been successful in the past should be maintained.

As valuable as the updated knowledge is, it will take some time and effort to incorporate it into our current child-rearing practices. As a parent you will find it challenging to develop a new pattern of functioning, a new way of relating, or a new form of disciplining that you yourself did not experience as a child. Indeed, the majority of your parenting practices come from your own childhood experiences and memories—and unless you have a new road map with new directions you will probably raise your child exactly like your parents raised you.

This does not necessarily mean that how your parents raised you was bad. The primary concern is that your parents probably used child—rearing practices based on the traditional major child-developmental theories that evolved from studies done on troubled—rather than successful, well-adapted—children and adults. In the past, researchers and child development theorists tried to determine what went wrong in their subjects' upbringing and early development that led to troubled adolescence and adulthood. These researchers primarily relied on adults' childhood memories for information. Such an approach, which was utilized with emotionally disturbed adolescents and adults and based solely on their memories, was distorted in numerous ways.

In contrast, research done in the last twenty years, and especially in the last ten years, has focused on healthy, successful children and their parents. Since these studies take place "in the present," they can provide a clearer, more precise view of what it is that children react to and how their responses depend on their own genetic and environmental contributions. This recent research has provided a much better understanding of the specific developmental capacities of a child, what is important in each stage of a child's development, how parents and a child respond to each other in the very early stages of development, and how these early parent-child interactions contribute to their ongoing, lifelong relationship.

I have written *Raising a Successful Child (The Manual)* especially for adults who are considering becoming parents, for new parents, and for parents of children up to age fifteen. Grandparents will also find this book useful in developing healthy, satisfying relationships with their grandchildren as well as in helping their own children—the parents of their grandchildren—develop new and better ways of parenting.

Chapter 1, "Building a Positive Relationship with Your Infant or Toddler," focuses on infants and very young children, specifically their capabilities and their need to develop a positive relationship with their parents. This chapter will help you understand the importance of verbal and physical contact, the amount of time you spend with your child, and the ongoing interactions that will serve as a relational baseline throughout your child's development.

Chapter 2, "Establishing a Playful Relationship with Your Child," emphasizes the importance of play and focuses on child rearing as a pleasurable experience. You will learn about the types of play that are important at different developmental stages and the various approaches you can use to establish and maintain a playful relationship with your child.

Chapter 3, "Developing Better Parenting Behaviors," addresses many of the common fears and misconceptions about parenting. It provides a wealth of material that you can use to formulate clear responses to your own fears as well as how to put your fears in perspective. As an adult you have numerous misconceptions that arise out of your own personal history as well as what others have told you. Also, you will have no lack of advice from family members, friends, and other sources on how to raise your child. Although much of this advice may be good-willed and informative, some of it may be based on another person's unique experience with his/her own child and will have no bearing whatsoever on your unique relationship with your own child.

Chapter 4, "Maintaining a Positive, Mutually Satisfying Relationship," details the basic, crucial ingredients in raising a successful child. This information will help you understand the issues you face as a parent in today's world, where parents are more isolated and have less support than ever before in history.

Chapter 5, "Using Discipline To Help Your Child Develop Self-Discipline," focuses on how to use discipline to produce positive results. I deliberately placed this chapter last to encourage you to read the rest of the book first. Once you thoroughly understand the underlying factors in developing a positive relationship and having fun with your child, discipline will take a backseat.

The final chapter, "Some Notes on Divorce", provide parents who are or will cross this bridge some guidelines to managing their relationships with their children.

Raising a Successful Child (The Manual) represents my accumulation of research, reading, introspection, and personal and professional experiences over the past twenty-five years. But the roots of this book go back even further, back to the questions I had as a child and the fantasies I had in relation to my own children. I hope that as you read the following chapters you will gain not only an understanding of infants' and children's needs but also of what you can do to effectively meet your child's needs. I also hope that the information in this book will help you examine your parenting practices and encourage you to develop new skills and new ways of self-management. Then you can create your own unique road map for raising your children in a way that helps them become capable, well-adjusted, success-oriented adults.

.

CHAPTER 1

BUILDING A POSITIVE RELATIONSHIP WITH YOUR INFANT OR TODDLER

Your relationship with your infant began many years before he/she was even conceived—it began when you were a child yourself. As you were growing up you probably fantasized about the time when you would have children of your own. You played "house" and acted out how you would treat your children—what you would say to them, what you would do for them, and even how you would discipline them. As an adolescent and young adult, you continued to look ahead to the time when you would become a parent.

Your childhood fantasies about parenthood play a key role in the relationship you have with your infant or toddler.[1] Another key factor is the quality of your experiences related to your child's conception, the course of pregnancy, and labor and delivery. What you thought and how you felt when you found out that you were (or your spouse was) pregnant, throughout the nine months of pregnancy, and during the actual birth process affects what you think and how you feel about your newborn infant.

The moment of birth is an extraordinary event both in your development as a person and in your child's development. For sure it was a time of excitement, and hopefully it was also a time of joy. No matter what you thought or felt when your child was born, you will never, ever forget that once-in-a-lifetime moment.

Beginning the Ongoing Process

As you move beyond your child's birth and begin living the daily realities of being a parent, keep in mind that your relationship with your child will develop over time, indeed over a lifetime. Building a positive relationship with your child will take a lot of consistent effort on your part in the days, weeks, months, and years to come. The everyday normal caretaking, child-rearing activities will naturally form an attachment—your parent-child relationship—between you and your child. The *quality* of that relationship depends on how you interact with your child when you are meeting his/her needs as well as when you "play" with your child.

Your past experiences have probably already given you all the "tools" you need to develop a positive, healthy relationship with your child. The next step is for you to learn to use these tools. That's what this book is all about. You will learn about your child's physical, neurological, and emotional needs at each stage of his/her development and how to meet those needs in ways that encourage your child to successfully mature into a responsible, independent, self-sufficient adult.

As a parent you shoulder the basic responsibility for meeting your child's needs, but building a positive, nurturing parent-child relationship also depends on your interaction with your child—how you respond to your child and how your child responds to you. Parents tend to respond to their children about one-half step beyond the child's chronological age,[2] which allows them to invite and encourage their children toward further development. For example, when your child takes his/her first step, you will probably step back, applaud that first step, and invite your child to take another and another. Within a very short time you will be inviting your child to walk farther and faster and then to run.

Your approval coupled with your invitation to your child to "take the next step" encourages your child to continue to develop and master skills.

Both you and your child will be excited about the successful achievement of each new skill, but as a parent you will also feel a certain sadness as your child progresses from one developmental stage to the next. You will realize that with each "step" a special moment has passed, a moment that can never be re-experienced. However, the inherent sadness you feel as you watch your child progress from a helpless infant completely dependent on you to an independent young adult does not stop you from inviting your child to continue to take the "next step." Just as adult birds instinctively push their fledglings out of the nest, you will instinctively invite and encourage your child to become more and more independent.

Your interaction with your child from his/her birth through early childhood greatly affects your child's personality, which will be well-formed by his/her third birthday. The information on the following pages will help you to understand what you can do to help your child successfully develop a healthy personality during this crucial formative period.

Hold and Love Your Infant

Perhaps one of the simplest and yet most important things you can do is to hold your infant. Research studies confirm that *infants thrive when they are physically held, stimulated, and touched.* It helps premature babies gain weight and healthy babies digest food.[3]

Physical contact also reduces stress, so whenever your infant cries, hold and soothe him/her. There is no such thing as a "spoiled baby" because an infant's neurological development is not advanced enough to even begin constructing ideas related to spoiling. I cannot stress enough how important it is for you to pick up and hold your infant in a soothing, calm manner whenever he/she is fearful, tense, stressed, or simply in need of comfort for whatever reason.

Research clearly shows that *infants whose parents respond in a sensitive manner and comfort them on a regular and consistent basis are much more likely to develop healthy attachments and a capacity for self-regulation quicker than infants who are not held or comforted.* Whatever your child receives from the external world becomes part of his/her experiences and is then available for his/her internal use. That is, a child who is responded to by consistent soothing and calming efforts, on behalf of their parents will learn to soothe, calm and regulate his/her own future experiences of distress. A child who is not offered such a kind and comforting response will have difficulties responding to his/her own internal distress, emotional unsettledness in a self-regulating fashion and will be at higher risk of future problems in self-management. Thus your child will gain the capacity to learn how to manage his/her feelings and to set rules and self-limits by experiencing external rules and limits that are provided in a soothing, regulating manner. The bottom line is that *your infant needs you to hold and love him/her a lot.*

Stimulate Your Infant's Senses

Historic theories on child development portrayed infants as being almost autistic[4] at times and having a "stimulus barrier"[5] to protect him/her from being overwhelmed by

even relatively minor stimuli from the surrounding environment. We now know however
that *infants are quite interested in their
environment and are capable of processing
stimuli visually as well as through touch-
ing, smelling, hearing, and tasting.* Indeed
it is very clear that infants are born <u>stimu-
lus seeking</u> — not stimulus avoidant.

Research indicates that infants from birth
to three days of age can see an average distance of approximately eight inches,[6] which
is the average distance from a woman's breast
to her face. Thus when an infant is suckling
at his/her mother's breast, he/she is able to
see his/her mother's face and visually learn
about her. It is this "mutual gaze" often
seen in pictures of a suckling infant and
mother that helps the infant differentiate
his/her mother from another woman. When bottle feeding, it is also important for parents
to make an effort to hold their babies close.

Also within the first few days of life,
an infant can differentiate his/her mother
from other people on the basis smell. Once
researchers established that head turning in
infants is a *voluntary* response, they placed
a breast pad from an infant's mother on one

side of the infant's head and the breast
pad from another woman on the other side.
Each infant in the study consistently turned
toward his/her mother's breast pad even when
the pads were switched from side to side.[7]
This study established that an infant can
recognize, separate, and differentiate his/
her mother from other people on the basis of
smell.

Research has also shown that an infant can
recognize his/her mother on the basis of
sound. In one study researchers recorded each
infant's mother and a another woman with a
similar voice both telling the same story.
They attached an electronic pacifier to two
tape recorders, one playing the tape of the
mother's voice and the other playing the
tape of the other woman's. The infant's rate
of sucking on the electronic pacifier would
determine which tape-recorded voice he/she
would hear. Previous studies had determined
that although sucking is a reflex, the rate
of sucking is voluntary. The researchers
found that each infant consistently sucked
the pacifier at a rate that would maintain
his/her mother's voice playing! Whenever the
infant's sucking slowed down or speeded up
to the point where the other woman's voice

cut in, the infant would quickly adjust his/her speed of sucking to hear his/her mother's voice again.

Studies have also determined what infants like to look at in their environment. Again using an electronic pacifier, researchers correlated each infant's rate of sucking with various images in a slide presentation. They found that infants sucked when they saw images that interested them. The one image which created the most consistent and significant response was the human face. That's why crib mobiles as well as toys and other objects for infants show the human face in one form or another. The marketplace has clearly stayed abreast of all of these current findings and manufacturers, are making a fortune.

Provide Social Contact and Interaction

As your infant's visual abilities develop so do his/her social capacities. By the time he/she is approximately three months old, your infant is almost on par with you in terms of his/her visual field, and he/she is then capable of initiating, maintaining, regulating, or stopping a social interaction simply on the basis of eye movement. *Indeed*, *the period from three to six months has been described as the human's most social time of life,*[8] *yet during this time he/she is relatively immobile and extraordinarily dependent on you and others to provide all his/her social interaction.* To help you understand your infant's situation, imagine yourself having been in an accident that broke your neck and all of your limbs, leaving you lying in a hospital bed in a full-body cast with your neck in traction and not being able to talk. The only way you can contact other people is with your eyes, which glare out from your cast. You are thrilled when someone comes by, leans down to look directly into your eyes, and talks to you—you are especially appreciative when the nurse asks you to blink once for additional pain medication. You quickly master the art of eye contact. Don't leave your infant without contact for any longer than you would want! This is especially important for day care providers to understand. Contact with infants during this period is crucial when they are awake, alert and calm. Simply responding when the infant cries or is in distress <u>fails</u> to meet the infant's <u>needs</u>.

Infants do the same thing. They learn to use their eyes to have contact with other people to satisfy their need for human relation-ships. You have probably experienced catching a glimpse of a baby looking at you and being *caught* in his/her line of vision. Videotapes of eye contact between infants and adults show that this social encounter begins with the infant widening his/her eyes followed by the adult widening his/her eyes in response. After the initial "entrapment" the infant will further engage the adult with a wide range of eye shifts that regulate the social interaction, which is a monumental develop-mental step for the infant. In response to the infant, you find yourself making all kinds of contortions with your face and perhaps making an array of sounds which you believe will hold the infant's attention.

As long as the infant is interested in you and finds you entertaining, he/she will main-tain eye contact, a pleasurable experience for both of you. Once the infant tires of "connecting" with you however, he/she will avert his/her gaze. You will probably try to regain contact with the infant through your repertoire of facial contortions and high pitched sounds, but to no avail—he/she has used his/her social powers to regulate the social encounter <u>to his/her own satisfaction</u>.

The only difficulties that arise in this social interaction come from the responses of parents who do not understand what their infant is doing, when he/she averts his/her gaze. An anxious parent may well perceive eye aversion as a rejection and feel hurt. A parent who is unsure and perhaps "needs" the infant's gaze for reassurance may "chase" the infant's gaze from one side of the crib to the other. An even more anxious parent may hold the infant's head still in order to try to maintain eye contact with him/her, but the infant will most likely simply shut his/her eyes to end the social encounter. *Parents and other adults need to understand that the infant is not deliberately acting defiant or oppositional in ending eye-contact social encounters; it is a normal part of the human developmental process.* In many ways it marks the beginning of social independence and must be understood as a dramatic developmental advance.

As such, be especially attentive to your infant's needs for significant social contact and interaction between the ages of three and six months. Provide sensory stimulation and other contact with people and the environment during times when he/she is awake, alert, and quiet. Also alert the other adults who take care of your child to his/her particular and significant need for stimulation and social contact during this developmental period.

Talk and Read to Your Young Child

Young children who are talked to, read to, and live in an atmosphere of verbal interaction and stimulation develop higher vocabularies than other children. These children also score higher on IQ tests compared to children who are not talked to as infants. These findings have been replicated so many times that they can be seen as a given.

While your infant's visual development takes place primarily between the ages of three and six months, his/her verbal skills continue to develop past six months of age. His/her visual world which has been shared with you will also begin to lose importance about six months of age. At this stage his/her interest shifts to developing fine motor skills by holding onto objects rather than just looking at them. Thus handheld objects may take on a significant amount of attention. However, they continue to be dependent on their adult caregivers for social interaction.

Although your six-month old baby or toddler may not be the most interesting conversationalist, your verbal interactions with him/her will pay off grandly. It really doesn't matter what you talk about with him/her—you can discuss anything and everything! You can recite the ABCs or introduce him/her to classical literature or geometric theorems if you'd like, but it's not necessary. *What matters the most is that you and others talk to your child on a consistent basis that allows them to develop and maintain human contact!*

Research has shown that infants do like to be talked to at times in baby-talk, something that adults seem to do automatically. Adults tend to raise the pitch of their voice and talk to infants in exaggerated tones, and infants tend to respond positively to such talk. Even so, it's a good idea to talk to your child in a regular tone of voice too. Infants seem to be attracted to the fluctuation between different tones and types of cadences in speech, and through the pleasure of speech interaction they will develop an ongoing sense of connectedness and relationship with you.

Focus on Forward Progress Instead of a Specific Time Range

You can find numerous checklists and graphs in books, magazines, and other sources that outline physical and neurological development and give time ranges for each developmental stage. Most of these informational materials are based on the same research, and as long as they were compiled after 1990 the information is probably up-to-date.

The most important thing to keep in mind is that there is always a range of "normal" time for a child to master a developmental task. For example, a child may learn to walk anywhere between the ages of nine and seventeen months. While a large number of children learn to walk by their first birthday, it is not unusual—and certainly not a reason to panic—if your child does not learn to walk until several months after his/her first birthday.

In addition to walking, many parents are concerned about when their child should be talking. While early speech correlates well with later academic success for girls, it does not correlate with later achievements for all boys—and relatively late speech development *does not* correlate at all with either academic success or lack of success for boys.

Thus, use the time ranges in the informational materials as a general guide, but do not become anxious if your child does not achieve a particular developmental level by a certain date. *Focus instead on inviting and encouraging your child to continue to develop his/her skills and move toward mastery of developmental tasks.* And if you are concerned that your child is not developing as he/she "should," contact your pediatrician for a professional evaluation and advice.

Expose Your Young Child to a Variety of Physical and Mental Tasks

Exposing your child to a variety of physical and mental activities will help ensure that he/she learns a wide range of fine and gross motor skills. Children who have not had exposure and experience with activities that require specific motor skills before the age of twelve may well have difficulty learning those skills later in life. It is not important for a child to master all sports/ skills as much as it is extremely important that they are exposed to a wide range of experiences that allows them to attain developmentally expected success in a wide range of motor skills. Further, while a child may portray a "talent" or advanced skills in an activity, pursuit or sport, it is very important that a child be introduced to additional activities/sports to insure a more well-rounded or balance of skills. The child may well continue to invest in the one preferred sport or may possibly find others that offer equal or greater enjoyment and success.

Fine motor skills involve small muscle movements such as holding a pencil, using a paintbrush, and manipulating small items with your fingers. Gross motor skills involve large muscle movements such as walking, running, balancing, and riding a bike. Fine gross motor skills tend to develop independently of each other, and your child will focus on one or the other at different times during his/her development. So when your child is learning to walk, which is a gross motor skill, that activity will take precedence—at least for a short time—over any efforts to manipulate small items, a fine motor skill. You don't need to worry that your child is falling behind in developing one skill or another—he/she will develop each skill in due course. Your child has the capacity to focus on developing one skill while the parts of his/her body that are not involved are "resting."

In addition to providing activities to help your child learn physical and athletic skills, be sure to also give your child opportunities to draw, paint, write, and experience music. Again, the goal at this early stage of your child's development is not to enable him/her to become a world-class athlete or artist but rather to help him/her develop fine and gross motor skills. If your child does not have the opportunity to develop these skills in the first eleven or twelve years of life, he/she may never fully master them or even want to attempt them.

Also introduce your child to a foreign language early in his/her life. Research has shown that a child's development, understanding, and capacity to learn a foreign language is optimum between the ages of two and seven. Children in Europe have the advantage of hearing and learning to speak multiple languages in early childhood, but most American children don't have that opportunity. Few American families speak a second language at home, and most public schools in the United States don't offer foreign language classes until the junior or senior-high grades! What is missing here? While there are perhaps numerous historical as well as financial explanations for our children not learning foreign languages early in life, the fact remains that unless your child is enrolled in a "special" program/school that addresses this, it will be up to you the parent to introduce your children to foreign languages early in life.

Develop a Healthy Emotional Relationship with Your Child

The emotional relationship that a parent has with his/her child isn't often discussed in parenting magazines or other publications. And you will find very few checklists to help you assess the quality of your parent/child relationship or how to develop a healthy relationship. A few theoretical constructs do exist however that can help you organize your thinking about your emotional relationship with your child.

The late child analyst and pediatrician David Winnicott coined the terms "good enough mother" and "good enough environment"[9] to emphasize that *there is no such thing as a "perfect" parent or environment.* Indeed, such perfection, if it did exist, would not be healthy for a child because he/she would never have an opportunity to develop any type of frustration tolerance and/or impulse control because they simply would not be needed. *A "good enough parent" provides a sense of safety, protection, dependability, and reliability in an environment that allows reality and various stimuli to be introduced at a rate compatible to the child's personality and capacities to adjust to them. A "good enough environment" protects against trauma entering from the outside world as well as both overstimulation and understimulation.*

Keep in mind that there is no "perfection" when it comes to parenting, and oftentimes

our minor failures
children to develop
frustration toleran
"less-than-perfect"
strive to function "
a healthy relationsh:
to have only "good er.
fect"—expectations of

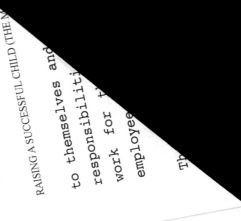

Base Your Relations.__μ on Acceptance, Respect, Consistency, and Reliability

If you handle yourself well as a parent and have a positive attitude toward your child you are establishing a "good enough" parent/ child relationship. *A healthy emotional relationship grows in an atmosphere of acceptance and respect underscored with consistency and reliability.* Indeed these are the crucial elements needed to develop trust with your child.

You are already familiar with these elements since they are the same ones you use to assess your relationships with other adults. You know that you can trust people who do what they say, are there when they say they will be, are consistent in their presentations

to you, and perform their
es responsibly. You want to
hese people, hire them as your
s, and maintain them for friends.

e same holds true for you and your child. Being consistent, reliable, and trustworthy will help you to develop a healthy parent/ child relationship in which your child will not only trust you, they will also learn to fashion their own interactions with you and others based on the model of functioning you provide. Never believe for a second that because your child is in an early stage of development that how you manage yourself in relationship to your child and with others doesn't make an impact. Simply understand that however you hope your child will behave in their future interactions with you and others is based on how you manage your paren- tal relationship with your child.

Assess the Ghosts in Your Nursery and Your Representational World

Selma Fraiberg, E. Adeson and V. Shapiro made a major contribution to child development literature when they wrote "Ghosts in the

Nursery."[10] In their article Fraiberg, Adeson and Shapiro noted that each parent brings with him/her an entire history of internal models of parenting and relating that will impact his/her relationship with his/her child. With these "ghosts" flying around in the nursery the parent begins to set his/her expectations of the child. These ghosts include our parents' and grandparents' attitudes and beliefs about how babies should be fed, how they should be disciplined, and a host of other parenting issues you may not have considered yet.

Your ghosts will influence your thinking, and if you are consciously aware of them you can evaluate these beliefs and attitudes and modify any potential negative impact they may have on your relationship with your child. If you are not consciously aware of these ghosts, they will still impact your parent/child relationship but perhaps in a destructive way. Be sure to become aware of the ghosts in your child's nursery so you can avoid replicating any unhealthy parenting practices.

In general, infant research has been conceptualized around the paradigm

$$MR \leftrightarrow [MB \leftrightarrow IB] \leftrightarrow IR$$

where M stands for Mother, I for Infant, B for Behavior, and R for the Representational World.[11]

The first studies focused on the behavior of the infant and yielded discoveries about infant development, motor skills development, and expectations for developmental growth based on the infant and his/her capacities. The focus then shifted to the interaction between the mother's behavior and the infant's behavior. These studies revealed information about who initiates what during the course of parent/child interactions including the fact that the infant, rather than the adult, controls social interactions when the infant is between three and six months of age.[12]

Later, scientific curiosity focused on why particular parents responded in the specific ways they did when their infant gave them cues. This led to studies on the internal representational world of the parents, what the infant means to them, and what they were thinking about—as well as the impact of their own history—when they responded to their infant. Additional research studied the infant's representational world including how an infant begins to develop memories and organize his/her own world around specific memories.[13]

Research on the mother's and father's representational world led to the following assessment method to help you understand the parental/grandparental ghosts in your nursery as well as your own representational world, all of which impact your interactions with your child. You can answer these questions both independently and jointly with your spouse:

Question 1: What does this child mean to me/us?

What your child means to you may require an extensive answer. Some children are seen as a replacement for a loss or as proof of masculinity and/or femininity on the parts of the parents. A child may also be seen as marital glue or some other type of individual or marital achievement. Parents who had difficulty conceiving and perhaps experienced a miscarriage may perceive their child to be a gift; if this is the parent's only or major perception of the child they may encounter problems with discipline as the child grows because it is extremely difficult to set limits on a "gift."

Most parents have multiple perceptions of their child, which is quite healthy. Indeed, the healthiest situation is having a rich, elaborate scheme of perceptions that fluctuates back and forth allowing the parent to see the child in a multitude of different ways. A parent who perceives his/her child in a singular, somewhat rigid way runs the danger of having an unhealthy, unchanging, inflexible parent/child relationship.

Question 2: What or how does having this child change my/our perception of myself/ourselves?

Having a child is going to change your life—there's no doubt about that. If this is your first child, he/she may change a number of situations in your life, especially your social life. A group of researchers in Italy also found that a mother's first child often serves as a symbol of a "loss of an irreplaceable status" because the mother is no longer a daughter to her mother but rather a mother to her own child. These kinds of life changes force developmental shifts for the adults involved and often become areas of significant struggle. These shifts can also bring welcome developmental advancement in the parent's life.

Question 3:   How do you see yourself as a mother or father?

Question 4:   How do you see your spouse as a mother or father?

Question 5:   How do you see yourself as a parent?

Question 6:   What in your past is likely to either positively or negatively impact your parenting?

Question 7:   What in your past would you like to repeat in parenting your own child?

Question 8:   What in your past would you like not to repeat in parenting your own child?

Question 9:   What in your spouse's past would you like to see him/her repeat in parenting your child?

Question 10: What in your spouse's past would you like him/her not to repeat in parenting your child?

Question 11: How can you and your spouse help each other avoid repeating unwanted parenting techniques?

Answering the above questions will help make you aware of the quality and type of emotional relationship you began to establish with your infant even before his/her birth. Your expectations, wishes, fantasies, and attitudes toward your child will continue to impact your lifelong parent/child relationship.

What Your Child Brings to Your Parent/Child Relationship

Your child, who is the product of years of fantasy, months of pregnancy followed by hours of labor and delivery, makes a major contribution to your emotional relationship with him/her. A complicated, painful pregnancy or birth can set the stage for understandable resentment on the part of the parents.

The first few days and weeks following your child's birth will also play a crucial role in your emotional relationship. Parents usually find it easy to form a positive, happy, attachment to a healthy infant who eats and sleeps well and responds positively to their efforts at soothing and regulating. These parents feel satisfied that they are doing a good job. On the other hand, parents of infants who have special needs, are not good eaters or sleepers, or have colic or other health problems often feel like failures at parenting.

Research studies indicate that infants who have low muscle tone and/or difficult temperaments often provide a major stimulus for postpartum depression and additional depression in their mothers.[14] Looking forward to the birth of a child and the joys of holding him/her only to have an infant who cries twelve to eighteen hours a day and does not respond to parenting efforts to soothe and regulate will tax even a parent who has a healthy sense of self-worth and self-esteem. Such situations understandably create anxieties and a sense of failure—as well as an atmosphere of fear and a shaken sense of self, all of which can negatively impact a parent's emotional relationship with his/her child.

In fact, many infants are oversensitive to touch, sight, smell, as well as other senses. Sometimes relatively quick, easy interventions can help diminish some of the negative impact of these situations. For example, an infant who is oversensitive to touch may be placed on a soft pillow while he/she nurses or is fed a bottle. This allows both parents to hold the baby, share a mutual eye gaze, and experience a pleasurable interaction with their infant.

Parents today have a wide range of interventions to help relieve problems on the part of the infant that can interfere with the development of a mutually satisfying parent/child relationship. In the past mothers who suffered postpartum depression were often considered the cause of depression and upset in their infants. Now we know that the parent/child interaction plays a role in both postpartum depression and other unsatisfying factors that negatively impact parent/child relationships.

Mismatches That Can Negatively Impact Your Parent/Child Relationship

Sometimes *temperamental/affective "mismatches"* between a parent and his/her infant or young child can negatively affect the entire history of the parent/child relationship. Both the parent and the infant may be quite healthy, adaptive, and well-functioning individuals, and neither of them is "bad." The difficulty stems from the fact that each is a different type of person. For instance, a parent who was an "easy" infant and a calm child who responded well to his/her own parenting, required little discipline, and enjoyed a wide range of successes may be "blessed" with a child who is somewhat high-energy as well as quite strong-willed. These parents often seek professional help in dealing with a child they believe may be hyperactive or other concerns that require a diagnostic evaluation. Quite often these are older parents who come home tired after a long day at work to a child who is ready to play for the next three to twelve hours. In these cases I always emphasize that *there is nothing wrong with either the parent or the child—they just have different temperaments, energy levels, etc.*

Of course the opposite situation also frequently occurs—a high-energy, strong-willed, hard-driven, very successful parent is "blessed" with a child who is calm and laid-back and has a noncompetitive temperament.

These parents often bring in their children for clinical assessment for depression and/or related conditions. Again, there is nothing wrong with either the parent or the child—the child simply does not meet the parent's expectations and/or fantasies about what their child "should be".

Unfortunately these mismatches can negatively affect the entire history of the parent/child relationship. Although neither party is "bad," the parent may see his/her child as unacceptable and the child may go through life feeling criticized and rejected. The high-energy child may be constantly told to "settle/calm down," while the calm, laid-back child may feel that he/she cannot keep up with his/her parent, doesn't have enough enthusiasm for family activities, and isn't able to "fill the old man's shoes."

You must learn to assess your child's individual temperament and energy level and realize that they are not going to change. Nor is your child's affective experience likely to change. Some children will always wear their feelings on their sleeve and be quick to respond—just like some adults, while other children—and adults—will always appear very stoic and nonresponsive no matter what the situation. Determine if you and your child are mismatched in any way, and be aware that any mismatch can create an unhealthy, unhappy parent/child relationship that may cause you to unconsciously tend to criticize your child throughout his/her development into adulthood and even beyond.

Another potential source of mismatch stems from how the parent and child "organize" their worlds. Some children and adults organize their perceptions and cognitive processes around details and become quite consumed by details, while others organize around the "general" and the "whole." A mismatched parent and child will find it very difficult to communicate well because one of them will always focus on the details and miss the big picture while the other will quickly become bored by having to listen to what he/she perceives to be unimportant details instead of just "getting on with it."

You can begin to assess your child's temperament, energy level, and affectivity from the time he/she is born by observing his/her cues—his/her types of cries and signals to be fed, changed, or held and soothed. As you grow in your understanding of your child, you will begin to relate to him/her as an individual rather than blindly relating to him/her as either a carbon copy of you or your fantasy of what a boy or girl baby "should be"!

My wife and I learned about our need to treat our daughter as her own person the day we brought her home from the hospital. As we looked down at her lying calmly on the couch, my wife said, "She's tired and needs a nap." I responded that I thought she was bored and needed to play, perhaps even going outside to get some fresh air. My wife and I then looked at each other and realized that we had, in fact, expressed what we wished for our own selves that very moment. We also realized we didn't have a clue about what our daughter wanted!

Fathers as well as Mothers Play Significant Roles in Parenting

I want to emphasize that all the information in this book applies to both parents—a child's mother as well as his/her father. Everyone seems to acknowledge the important role that a mother plays in raising an infant or young child, but few acknowledge that *a father's involvement is absolutely crucial for a child to develop a healthy self-esteem and to function well in other areas of development.* Research has shown that children who have positive relationships with their fathers develop better social skills and not only score higher on IQ tests but also perform better academically throughout their development.[15]

A daughter who has a positive relationship with her father will have a higher level of self-esteem than a daughter without a a positive relationship will be able to attain. The sense of security provided by a daughter's positive relationship with her father will give her an ongoing sense of competence and a capacity for assertiveness that is unmatched by any other force.

Also, fathers who are actively engaged with their infants and young children are less likely and at significantly less risk to be abusive either sexually or physically.[16]

If you are a man and have read the above paragraphs, you will no longer be able to father a child without becoming actively involved in his/her welfare because you will be know- ingly neglecting his/her needs.

Tips on Building a Positive Relationship with Your Infant or Toddler

- Remember that your relationship with your child will develop over time—a lifetime.
- How you interact with your child when you are meeting his/her needs as well as when you "play" with your child will determine the *quality* of your parent-child relationship.
- You automatically encourage your child to continually develop and master new skills by approving his/ her accomplishments and immediately inviting him or her to "take the next step."
- As you watch your child progress from a helpless infant to an independent young adult, you will feel some sadness—but that will not

stop you from inviting your child to continue to develop new skills.

- Your interaction with your child during the first three years of his/her life greatly affects the development of his/her personality.
- One of the most important things you can do for your child is to hold and love him/her *a lot*. To help your child develop healthy relationships and the capacity for self-regulation, you must pick up and hold him or her in a soothing, calm manner whenever he/she is fearful, tense, stressed, or simply in need of comfort for whatever reason.
- Stimulate your child's senses to help him/her learn about you and his/her environment through sight, touch, smell, hearing, and taste.
- Your child especially needs social contact and interaction between the ages of three to six months, and he/she is extraordinarily dependent on you and others to meet those needs.

- Talk and read to your child on a consistent basis to help him/her develop and maintain human contact and to increase his/her vocabulary and IQ.
- Focus on inviting and encouraging your child to continue to develop his/her skills rather than worrying about whether or not he/she is mastering skills according to a "normal" time range.
- Expose your child to a variety of physical and mental activities to help ensure that he/she learns both fine and gross motor skills.
- Remember that there is no such thing as a "perfect" parent or "environment." Strive to be a "good enough" parent who provides a "good enough" environment and has "good enough" expectations of your child.
- Assess and deal with the parental and grandparental "ghosts" and aspects of your representational world that may negatively impact your relationship with your child.

- Be aware that problems related to pregnancy and the birth of your child as well as your child him/herself can interfere with the development of a mutually satisfying parent/child relationship. Seek professional help to address and relieve these problems.

- Determine if your child has a temperament, energy level, or affective experience that is the opposite of yours and what you can do to minimize any mismatch negatively affecting your parent/child relationship.

- Remember that a father's involvement is absolutely crucial for a child to develop a healthy self-esteem and to function well in other areas of development.

- You can nurture the development of a healthy emotional relationship with your child by surrounding him/her with an atmosphere of acceptance and respect underscored with consistency and reliability.

CHAPTER 2

ESTABLISHING A PLAYFUL RELATIONSHIP WITH YOUR CHILD

Play is the glue that binds ongoing relationships, yet parents generally tend to pay little attention to learning how to play with their child. Parents usually assume that play will come naturally to both their child and themselves. I believe that play is too important to be left to chance.

Knowing how to play with your child and enjoying playing with your child will not only foster a lifelong, strong, positive parent-child relationship, but it will also help your child to develop moral values as well as the motor, social, and communication skills needed for success in all areas of life. In addition, if you play with your child—and especially if you enjoy playing with him/her, you will develop a mutually satisfying relationship, and that positive relationship will minimize issues and concerns about discipline.

Playing Develops Motor Skills

Play contributes to—and perhaps may be the most important contributor to—the development of motor skills. This includes both specific fine and gross motor skills as well as general motor/neurological development. Fine and gross motor skills develop independently of each other, and research has shown that unless a child has been introduced to or gained mastery over a certain range of both kinds of skills in the first ten years of his/her life, he/she is unlikely to develop those skills later. Therefore, to help your child fully develop all of his/her motor skills you should provide a wide range of activities and opportunities for mastering a number of skills very early on. And one of the easiest and most fun ways to do that is through play. (For more information about the development of specific motor skills, see "Expose Your Young Child to a Variety of Physical and Mental Tasks" on page 38).

Parents often unconsciously or thoughtlessly believe that children will pick up all the motor skills they need by themselves, especially if appropriate "play" objects or equipment are provided. But simply placing a ball in the playroom or setting up a drawing table does not ensure that your child will pick up, throw, or kick a ball or draw a picture. Parking a bicycle inside your house, on the front porch, or in the garage does not ensure that your child will learn to ride it. You must interact with your child and participate in providing learning opportunities for him/her.

You must take the time to introduce your child to an activity when he/she is developmentally ready for the task, and you must continue to support your child's engagement in the task especially when he/she experiences failure in the learning process. If you don't provide instruction or support, your child may avoid trying a new activity out of fear of failure and/or due to his/her temperament, which may not be outgoing enough to engage in tasks in which he/she does not feel confident.

You must participate in your child's play and in the development of a wide range of skills to ensure that he/she has a well-rounded opportunity for engaging in these tasks at the appropriate time in his/her developmental growth. Always keep in mind however that your child will develop at his/her own pace. Focus on inviting and encouraging him/her to continue to develop his/her skills rather than worrying about whether or not he/she is mastering skills according to a "normal" time range. (For more information about time ranges, see "Focus on Forward Progress Instead of a Specific Time Range" on page 37.

Playing Develops Social Skills

Some children seem to be "wired" for social skills. They appear to be very social in nature, and they have a temperament and disposition set toward engagement with others in satisfying, pleasing ways. Other children may appear anxious and less competent in social interactions and the development of social skills.

The emphasis in the development of social skills needs to be on "skills," things that can be taught. Even though some children may seem to intuitively know these skills, the vast majority of children need their parents (and other adults) to teach them. *By teaching your child social skills, you will help him/her learn to interact pleasantly and cooperate with others, find pleasure in competition, grow in self-confidence, and gain competence in maintaining and regulating self-esteem.* Again, remember that your child will develop social skills at his/her own pace and the age ranges mentioned in the paragraphs below are just general guidelines.

Your child experiences the "most social time of life" when he/she is between approximately three and six months old (see "Provide Social Contact and Interaction for Your Infant" on page 31). This develop-mental period provides the ideal time for you not only to develop a positive emo-tional attachment with your child but also to begin engaging him/her in a sequence of activities that will contribute to his/her pleasure in living. During this time your child will take great pleasure in imitative games, such as making faces at him/her and imitating his/her face in return. This is also the time when you can physically play with your child in pleasurable ways that bring shrieks of joy that you will forever remember. While your child may not recall specific play experiences, these pleasurable interactions and learning opportunities lay down a strong foundation for your ongoing playful relationship.

Make the most of this early social developmental period because, like every other developmental period in your child's life, it will not be replicated. *This is a once-in-a-lifetime opportunity for you to engage your child in interactions where the entire focus and goal is to achieve mutual pleasure.* Freely engage in all kinds of activities with your child during this period of time without concern about teaching him/her specific skills—just have fun with him/her. Talk freely to your young child, pick him/her up often and playfully show him/her the world, and invite him/her to touch things. Remember: The goal is for your child to experience pleasure in interacting with you.

Playing Develops Communication Skills

Play not only helps children learn motor and social skills, but it also helps them learn communication skills. In fact, children use play to communicate. They play out (act out) events in an effort to master developmental milestones and challenges as well as to alleviate anxieties and overcome fears. You will find it exciting to watch your child communicate through play. Although some play may be "richer" than others in depicting your child's internal psychological life, all play will help your child deal with the internal aspects of his/her functioning.

The role of play in speech development began when your child began babbling and cooing as an infant. Your infant delighted you by making these sounds, and in turn he/she was delighted by your response, which served to strengthen your parent-child relationship and also to initiate the process of language development. Not long after your child began to communicate in words, he/she began to develop his/her own unique phrases, style of communication, and the creation of new words. These new words sometimes stem from difficulties in proper enunciation, but they may also reflect your child's conscious, creative efforts to play with words and use them in different contexts, which gives him/her great pleasure and also helps him/her master a range of skills.

As with other skills, your child requires many and varied opportunities to try out various sounds and words so he/she can master the intricacies of communication and become competent in these skills. Also, as with other skills, the responsibility falls on you to provide a wide range of play activities that encourage your child to interact with others so that he/she can try out and perfect his/her communication skills.

Play activities will also give your child the opportunity to communicate his/her anxieties and fear. Your child may repeatedly play out a scene until he/she has mastered a specific issue, concern, or fantasy inherent in the scene. Don't be concerned about this repetitive play—it is a normal part of childhood. Your child has his/her own internal ideas, fantasies, and beliefs as well as external role models to incorporate into his/her play, and observing your child at play may give you a picture of his/her perceptions of his/her social environment. Child therapists have long recognized that play provides both conscious and unconscious means for a child to organize and understand his/her world and for observers to understand a child's fears and anxieties.

Allow your child to take the lead in play activities and try not to interfere even if you become anxious about a theme that he/she is playing out. Instead of interrupting your child's play and redirecting his/her activity to help him/her avoid what you believe to be undesirable and/or painful anxieties or fantasies, just observe his/her play. Use the opportunity to understand more fully your child's concerns, perceptions, and fears and to discover unique creative aspects of your child's internal world.

Your child may also play out his/her dreams both in active play and through play with objects. Play activities allow your child to recall internal struggles, master a wide range of fears, and separate reality from nonreality. Your child needs the opportunities play provides to create new ideas and manage a large number of issues related to his/her daily life.

By watching your child in various play activities, you will learn much about his/her interests and beliefs. By playing with your child in an activity that he/she leads and you do not judge in any way, you will participate in his/her development processes. This will help your child to feel comfortable about communicating with you later when his/her interactions become more verbal, which sets the foundation for healthy, open communication in your lifelong parent-child relationship. If you don't participate in your child's play activities, he/she would probably still grow up with a capacity for verbal interaction, but he/she may feel inhibited about communicating his/her internal experiences to you. Show your child early on that you are very interested in knowing about his/her fears, dreams, and struggles by playing with him/her in nonintrusive, nondirective ways.

Playing with Objects

Somewhere between six months and a year, your child will become attracted to objects. During this period your interaction with your child will begin to focus on shared experiences of exploring new objects, playing with them, manipulating them, and using them to develop a range of fine and gross motor skills.

As your child approaches his/her first birthday, he/she will probably be crawling and perhaps walking from object to object in a room. At this stage your child will take absolute pleasure in mastering fine and gross motor skills, and his/her pleasure will be heightened whenever you participate in the joy he/she finds in successfully manipulating a toy and/or his/her own body. The applause you give your child on his/her newfound abilities and capacities will greatly contribute to the development of his/her self-esteem.

Most children take their first steps in a direction away from their parent(s), which marks their first movement toward independent functioning. This introduces a range of anxieties for both you and your child. While you may find absolute joy in watching your child develop new skills, you may also feel a sense of sadness about losing a special dependence and closeness.

When your child is between one and two years old, he/she will fully master a wide range of fine and gross motor skills, and he/she will want to share every newfound ability and discovery with you. Your child will probably be so excited at times that he/she will take you by the hand and pull you toward whatever it is that he/she has discovered, perhaps something as ordinary as an object on the floor. What your child wants to show you doesn't really matter—what matters most is sharing the excitement with you. These spontaneous child-parent interactions play a key role in the development of a playful relationship with your child. Expect these interactions and be open and willing to participate fully in these shared emotional experiences.

This parent-child "affective sharing" (the sharing of feelings) connected with objects as well as the mutual exploration of objects is especially crucial when your child is between twelve and twenty-four months old. During this time you should introduce your child to new activities as well as new sights and sounds to encourage him/her to explore his/her full range of senses. Let your child "help" in the kitchen—it may be messy, but he/she will find great pleasure in exploring his/her sense of touch and taste.

More than anything else your child needs you to be available to him/her during this important developmental period. Keep in mind though that parent availability means much more than just being physically present with your child—it means setting time aside every day specifically to play with him/her. It means *devoting* time to interact with your child daily during his/her waking hours in the same way you devote your time to a professional relationship or project in anticipation of future success.

When your child is between two and three and a half years old, he/she will begin parallel and imitative play. Parallel play refers to two or more children playing independently in the same room. The only interaction between the children may occur when one child notices a toy that another child has and tries to get that toy to increase his/her own pleasure. Parallel play simply means that the children are able to play in the same room in a cooperative manner without arguments and/or difficulties.

Imitative play refers to one child engaging in an activity and another child—or a number of children—observing and then imitating him/her. This sometimes happens when one child begins to cry. Other children in the room commonly react by crying themselves due to either imitating or empathizing with the first child. Crying elicits an empathic response from infants more often than any other noise.

Role Playing

Also between the ages of two and three and a half, your child may begin—and before long become very adept at—assigning roles to be acted out with relative perfection during play. Your child may assign roles to you and other adults as well as to his/her siblings and other children. As long as the role player(s) performs satisfactorily—which may border on perfection, the interaction between the child and the role player(s) remains joyful. Difficulty arises however when the role player(s) do not perform satisfactorily or become tired of the roles and either change the roles or walk away from the activity. At this developmental stage your child is not concerned about whether or not you or other role players are enjoying the interaction. It is a time of healthy narcissistic development in which your child will "use" other people to perform certain functions in order to achieve his/her own pleasure.

Note that this is a *healthy* period of narcissistic development, and it *does not forecast* any type of inappropriate narcissistic behavior later in your child's life. Adults who continue behaving in this infantile narcissistic way however will experience a range of difficulties in their interpersonal relationships.

After your child turns four, he/she will begin to appreciate shared rules, the concept of things being fair or unfair, and the understanding of taking turns. At this point you may be able to play very simple board games with your child and engage him/her in a beginning competitive spirit. But don't be dismayed if your four-year-old has difficulty accepting losses or even traumatically reacts to losing. This simply means that your child needs less-competitive activities until he/she develops a stronger sense of confidence and positive self-esteem so he/she can lose and experience frustration and disappointment without becoming depressed and losing his/her sense of self-worth.

Until your child portrays a level of self-management high enough to deal successfully with losing, he/she will continue to have difficulty with almost any kind of competitive activity. You can help your child increase his/her level of self-management by playing games in which there are no losers and everybody wins. This allows your child to share in the joy of others winning without "losing face" him/herself.

If your child continues to have difficulty losing by the time he/she reaches age five or six, you can help foster positive self-management by playing games in which success comes from losing and/or from managing losing in a socially acceptable way. At the end of the game you can even reward the "best loser" for his/her positive participation as well as his/her positive self-management.

Your own self-management of losing will provide a role model for your child. If your child sees you engaging in an activity and losing without portraying extreme disappointment and displeasure at your performance, he/she will tend to imitate your socially acceptable behavior. In this area your behavior, as well as your underlying attitudes, contribute more to your child's capacity to manage losing than any other factors.

Beginning at age five or six, your child may be able to successfully participate in group activities and enjoy a large-group experience. Some parents enroll their children in team sports at this age, but many children need more time to develop the skills necessary to succeed in activities that involve group interaction and group success and/or failure. You may want to wait until your child is seven or eight years old before signing him/her up for team activities.

By the time your child turns five or six, he/ she will be ready to participate in a wide range of physical, intellectual, artistic, and musical activities that will continue to help him/her master both fine and gross motor skills. By this age your child probably also will have progressed from interacting with just one person to interacting with two or more people in activities that involve coop- eration, sharing, taking turns, and competi- tion.

Understanding Your Developmental Perceptions about Play

Our conscious and unconscious perceptions about play tend to follow a developmen- tal sequence. At first, children play freely without concern or even notice what they are doing, and many adults perceive play as the thing children do all day. At this early stage play is not judged—it is simply accepted and expected by both children and adults.

This blissful period ends relatively early in life however once the distinction is made between "play" and "work." Depending on the culture and the belief system of the family, this separation of play and work may come as early as two years of age or whenever the child is assigned work to do and a role to fulfill. The underlying assumption appears to be that work is not supposed to be fun, and therefore pleasure becomes equated with play and nonpleasure with work. While adults may tell children that they should enjoy work, these same adults may daily complain about their work, which sends children a mixed message.

Once the dichotomy of play as pleasure and work as nonpleasure has been introduced, children and adults tend to perceive play as an interference that must be tolerated. As a child grows older parents tend to say, "He/she must have some time to play after school" or "He/she must have a bit of playtime every day." It becomes a matter of scheduling some "downtime" as if play were an important necessity of life but one that could be satisfied in some small portion of a day. This perception causes problems when the portion of the day allotted to play becomes smaller and smaller as the child gets older. The perception then becomes that play is an almost absolute waste of time, and the word "play" takes on a derogatory connotation as in the common commands "Stop playing around!" or "You can't play until you finish all your work."

These perceptions of play as a luxury and work as drudgery and necessity can foster a fear of growing up and/or a lack of interest in even thinking about the future. If a child perceives adulthood as a time in life devoid of any pleasure, he/she will have very little motivation to grow up. Many adolescents today hang on to childish interactions because they don't realize that young adulthood, middle adulthood, and old age do in fact include pleasurable activities. As a result, adolescents tend to refuse to engage in tasks, such as a job, that might bring them pleasure over the long run.

It is crucial that you as a parent assess your own attitudes toward work and play as well as the perceptions about work and play that you may be communicating to your child. It is also crucial that you do *not* define play as a waste of time if you want your child to look forward to developmental success and be confident that he/she will enjoy a lifetime of pleasurable activities. Be sure to play with your child in a positive way that encourages the development of a continuum of healthy, positive perceptions about both play and work.

This continuum of perceptions begins with nontask-related play activities that are simply for personal pleasure and leads to:

— task-related play activities that involve cooperative interaction

— task-related play activities that involve end mastery

— play activities that include pleasurable aspects as well as some social benefit

— play activities directed at maintaining personal existence

— play activities directed at developing and contributing to the pleasurable existence of others

— play activities that fulfill some level of self-actualization.

While some play activities will provide more pleasure than others, provide activities that will help your child understand that growing up is a progression toward fulfillment of fantasies and dreams as well as opportunities to enjoy ongoing pleasurable experiences. This will help offset his/her fears that as he/she gets older life will become filled with nonpleasurable activities, including work.

How To Play with Your Child

Research has shown that mothers play with their children differently than fathers do. Mothers tend to use more toys and concrete types of games, while fathers tend to physically involve themselves in play and encourage physical activities. Fathers are also more willing to let a child out of their sight than mothers. In fact, a father may let a baby crawl twice as far as a mother will before retrieving him/her. When a child confronts a novel situation that includes a dog, stranger, or new toy, ---mothers instinctively move closer to the child as if to offer reassurance, while fathers tend to stay back and just observe how the child is handling the situation.

Your child needs *both* you and your spouse to participate in play activities so that he/she will have a wide range of experiences and opportunities to develop fine and gross motor skills as well as social and communication skills. Recognize which activities you tend to prefer and challenge yourself to engage in activities that don't come "naturally" to you.

Whether you are the mother or the father, make time to play with your child. Keep in mind that simply being in the same room as your child doesn't count—you must devote time to playing with your child. Even though you may have an extremely busy work schedule, you have chosen to be a parent and the most important work you have to do at this point in your life is raising a successful child. Schedule time to play with your child on a daily and/or weekly basis and invest yourself in the scheduled time just as you would invest in a business obligation. Don't cancel these scheduled times or "blow them off"—your investment in your child's development not only will help avoid having to invest in a wide range of mental-health services later, but it will also yield invaluable, lifelong benefits for both you and your child.

Engage your child in:

—*child-initiated activities* in which you allow your child to select or create the activity or game and you follow without interjection of your own fantasies and/or wishes and without interrupting the activity because you find it distasteful or boring. It is very important that you simply follow your child's lead in these activities. It is also very important that you provide the opportunity every day for your child to initiate an activity and define it on his/her own for a limited time period, perhaps for as long as an hour. Your capacity to encourage and participate in child-initiated activities will serve you well in establishing a sound, playful relationship with your child.

—*joint-initiated activities* that may be defined initially by your child and expanded by you to challenge his/her developmental mastery of skills or to create a more exciting activity. These activities provide an opportunity to collaborate with your child and share mutual pleasure.

—*parent-introduced activities* that include both physical and intellectual activities/

games you believe will bring pleasure to your child, are important for your child to learn for one reason or another, or will teach a new skill. These activities may involve sports or the arts as well as the discovery of new places such as a playground or neighborhood. The skills involved in these activities run the gamut from physical to intellectual and social. These activities give you the opportunity not only to teach your child but also to serve as a role model for him/her in the areas of judgment, anticipation of consequences, impulse control, frustration tolerance, social interaction, and moral development. Engaging your child in these activities will encourage him/her to develop the functions and skills he/she needs to successfully adapt to his/her changing world as he/she matures.

During play activities you serve as a role model for your child, and he/she will learn the "proper" way to act from you. Keep in mind that if you tell your child to act a certain way and then role model a different behavior, your child will tend to do as you do, not as you say. As a parent you live in the proverbial fishbowl, and your child will take special note of your actions while you are playing with him/her.

Many parents express concern about where to take their children and which specific activities to introduce. The answers to these questions depend primarily on your child's abilities and talents. You probably have myriad play options available where you live ranging from hiking, swimming, skiing, and horseback riding to painting, attending concerts, and visiting museums. In addition, you can choose simpler activities such as playing catch, baking cookies, playing with dolls, computer games, watching DVDs, and flying a kite as well as imagination games in which you allow your child to take the lead. Whatever play activities you and your child participate in, remember the importance of diversity. Your child needs to successfully experience as wide a range of activities as possible in order to foster interest as well as competence in a number of areas.

Also remember the importance of moderation and don't allow your child to become obsessed with one activity to the exclusion of others. Sometimes an obsession develops when a child feels the pure joy of success and is motivated to repeat the success-giving activity. Other times a child may repeat a success-giving activity out of fear of trying something new and risking failure. Still other times a child may obsessively repeat an activity because he/she perceives it pleases his/her parent(s). In this situation the child may have identified and feels confident about something that is guaranteed to engage the parent in a pleasurable way. It may be related to the parent's own previous success at that particular activity and thus the parent can easily identify with the activity and show pride in the child's accomplishment. *Always keep in mind that the primary goal of parenting is to provide a wide range of activities and encourage and support the child's participation in activities he/she finds interesting.*

Try to imagine the ideal day for you and your child. Consider the physical, intellectual, emotional, and social activities that would directly benefit your child's development. You may come up with several options for your ideal day centered around a variety of activities that will give your child the play opportunities he/she needs not only to develop his/her skills but also to develop a playful relationship with you based on a history of shared pleasurable experiences.

Tips on Establishing a Playful Relationship with Your Child

Note: Always keep in mind that your child will develop at his/her own pace. Provide a wide range of play opportunities and focus on inviting and encouraging him/her to continue to develop his/her skills, and don't worry about whether or not he/she is mastering skills according to a "normal" time range.

- To help your child fully develop all of his/her fine and gross motor skills, provide a wide range of play activities and opportunities beginning in early infancy.
- Simply providing appropriate play equipment is not enough; you must participate in your child's play activities and encourage him/her when he/she experiences failure during the learning process.
- The primary focus of play activities is to achieve mutual

pleasure. This sets the foundation for a lifelong mutually satisfying parent-child relationship.

- Provide play opportunities that encourage your child to explore the full range of his/her senses.
- Make yourself available to your child by scheduling daily playtime with him/her. *Devote* this time to him/her.
- Remember that you serve as a role model for your child during play activities. Your child will tend to do as you do, not as you say.
- Assess your own attitudes about work and play, and strive to communicate to your child that play is very important and that work can be pleasurable.
- Be aware of the differences in the way fathers and mothers play with their children. Challenge yourself to play with your child in ways that don't come "naturally" to you so that you will provide the wide range of activities he/she needs

to fully develop his/her motor, social, and communication skills.

- Participate freely and often with your child in child-initiated, joint-initiated, and parent-initiated activities.
- Explore the full range of play activities available to you and your child. Remember the importance of both diversity and moderation.

CHAPTER 3

DEVELOPING BETTER
PARENTING BEHAVIORS

Many parents believe that the way their parents raised them is "good enough" for their own child, and they do things for and to their child without thinking. That's a big mistake. You *must* assess the value of your mother's and father's parenting behaviors before you do the same things for and to your own child to ensure that you don't inadvertently and unnecessarily cause your child to feel insecure, frustrated, and anxious.

To unquestioningly follow your parents' behaviors is to act like the proverbial newlyweds who decided to follow the wife's family's custom of having pasta for dinner every Thursday evening. Every Thursday they brought out the largest pot they had and cooked about three pounds of pasta, and every Thursday they ended up with more pasta than the two of them could eat. After a couple of years the husband finally said, "You know, we never ever eat all the pasta we cook on Thursday nights. There is no reason for us to cook three pounds of pasta for the two of us. So why do we keep doing it?" His wife replied, "Well, this is the same size pot and the same amount of pasta that my mother cooked every Thursday night when I was growing up."

Don't unquestioningly follow your parents' behaviors. Think about what you are going to do for or to your child before you do it. Instead of automatically doing what your parents did, determine if their parenting techniques nurtured your physical, emotional, and mental development and strengthened your parent/child relationship. Also use the information in this book to help you understand your child's needs at various stages of his/her development and what is needed to meet those needs. Then decide which techniques, perhaps some of your parent(s)' in combination with new ones described in this book and other sources of parenting information, will best meet your child's individual needs so that you can give your child something better than your parents gave you.

Act Rather Than React

At one time or another all of us spontaneously do or say things without fully understanding why we did or said them. Something "triggered" or "pushed our button" to unconsciously act in a particular way without thinking—we reacted rather than acted in these situations. Our individual triggers or buttons, which can send us into a rage, depression, and/or excitement, are rooted in our early developmental history as well as our background and our experiences in various social relationships.

In addition, each of us has a range of personal memories that remind us of pleasant and unpleasant experiences. When we consciously recall our memories, they can change our mood dramatically, which will affect the way we behave in the present. Quite often when a new mother or father feels stressed, they become anxious about how to handle a parenting situation. They think back to how their own parents handled a similar situation, and instead of exploring optional parenting techniques they resort to doing what their own parent(s) did for or to them. They simply repeat their own childhood experiences without considering the particular needs of their own child and how to best meet them in the current situation. Sometimes our remembered experiences and "triggered" responses provide positive parenting behaviors and motivate us to act in soothing, nurturing ways, but at other times our automatic responses replicate undesirable, detrimental behaviors.

To avoid unconsciously replicating potentially harmful parenting behaviors, become aware of your automatic responses. Monitor what you do for and to your child and look for behaviors that replicate your mother's or father's behaviors. Stop doing things just because your own parent(s) did them, objectively assess your parent(s)' behaviors as well as new techniques, and then act in the most responsive, positive, nurturing way that you can.

Adjust for Temperamental/Affective Mismatches

Keep in mind that everyone has his/her unique temperament and affect, and temperamental/affective mismatches create parenting challenges (see "Mismatches That Can Negatively Impact Your Parent/Child Relationship" on page 52. If you and your child have opposite (e.g., high/low-energy level, emotional/rational reactions to stress, competitive/

noncompetitive attitudes, or expressive/passive personality styles, temperaments and affects, you may sometimes feel at a loss about how to respond to your child's behavior or how to shape his/her behavior in a positive way. Keep in mind that your natural tendency—especially if you feel stressed—will be to replicate what your parents did for and to you, but these behaviors will probably not have a positive impact on your child due to your differences in personality, temperament, and changing cultural nuances.

Remember that if you and your child are "mismatched," *there is nothing wrong with either you or your child*—you just have different temperaments and affects. Assess your own as well as your child's temperament and affect and develop parenting techniques that will help your child continue to grow and reach his/her full potential as an individual.

Give Your Child Something Better

Accept the challenge of determining the best ways of handling parenting situations rather than falling back on what your parents did to or for you. That way you won't resort to spanking your child in exasperation simply because you "did not know what else to do" or "it seemed like the only thing left to do."

Especially strive to provide a relaxed, supportive, positive home environment, which may be vastly different from what you experienced as a child. If you have a positive rather than a negative or judgmental attitude toward your child, you will increase his/her self-esteem and self-confidence, two key components in your child's current as well as future successes. You will also lay a strong foundation for a positive, enjoyable parent/child relationship that will continue to strengthen in the years to come.

Beware of Your Envy

Even though consciously and rationally you may want to "give your child something better" than what your parents gave you, unconsciously your natural feelings of envy may stop you from parenting your child in "better" ways. Feelings of envy may unconsciously motivate you to replicate your mother's and father's parenting behaviors so that your child won't "get more" emotionally and/or materialistically than you got as a child.

Many parents say that they "work hard to give their child something better" or "they want their child to have it better than they did." But when they "give" something to their child they say, "You better appreciate this," "I worked awfully hard to give this to you," or "I never had anything like this when I was growing up," all of which tend to reduce the child's pleasure in receiving the gift. These parents are really saying, "What was good enough for me should be good enough for you."

Parents also express their envy in more subtle ways, such as working extensive hours and giving their children little of their time or energy. These parents often complain about their own fathers or mothers working all the time while they were growing up, yet they are replicating this unpleasant behavior. Today's parents who work all the time tend to be extremely successful financially and provide their children with every materialistic item, while their own parents probably had to work long hours just to make ends meet. The result is the same, however—the children experience loss, loneliness, frustration, and resentment.

When I served as the clinical director of an inpatient psychiatric program for adolescents, my staff and I worked very hard to provide a safe place where these children felt comfortable and at ease so that they would freely talk about and explore the difficulties that brought them to the hospital. One day during an occupational therapy session our patients let us know that we had succeeded in providing a safe haven for them. They painted T-shirts and on the back wrote the name of the hospital with "Country Club" after it. My staff and I took that as an extraordinary compliment to our ability to make these troubled young people feel accepted and cared for, but some of our patients' parents had a very negative response. They told us that they did not want their children to be in a "country club" and they were not paying for their children to be in a "country club." They seemed to want their children to "suffer" to some degree in the hospital, perhaps either in retaliation for the way the adolescents had made them suffer or out of envy that their troublemaking adolescents felt that they were living in a country club when the parents were not.

Whenever you feel excessively envious or resentful that your child "has it better" than you did as a child, stop and question both your response and your parenting behaviors. Reaffirm your goal of developing and using parenting techniques that have a positive impact on your child and that build a positive, lifelong parent/child relationship.

Don't Worry about Spoiling Your Child

There is no such thing as a spoiled baby! The idea is simply preposterous. The belief that picking up a baby every time he/she cries will spoil him/her shows a profound misunderstanding of the nature and developmental capacities of babies. Current research confirms that crying serves a range of functions for infants including communication, release of tension, and pleas for help.

Your child's crying does indeed serve a purpose, but that purpose is *not* manipulation. Your child cries in an effort to connect with you or another human being and to receive help in relieving the discomfort of hunger, other physical conditions, and/or a sense of aloneness (see "Hold and Love Your Infant" on page 27).

As a form of communication, crying evokes a range of feelings in parents. Within a week or two of their child's birth, new parents begin to "read" or interpret their child's different cries. They soon learn to differentiate hunger and discomfort cries from those prompted by fear or loneliness. Ignoring your child's cries and not responding to his/her attempts to enlist your help in meeting his/her needs quickly sends your child into a state of panic and psychological fragmentation. *If you do not respond to your child's cries in a reasonable, responsive, nurturing manner, he/she will begin to lose faith and trust in his/her home environment.*

Responding consistently and reliably to your child's cries will help him/her to develop trust and faith in you and others who care for him/her. This eventually leads to trust and faith in him/herself and the development of frustration tolerance and impulse control. Once your child trusts you to respond to his/her cries for help, he/she will be able to wait a while longer to be fed—both literally and symbolically.

You can never show your child too much concern and affection! Answering your child's cries in a reasonable, consistent way will build a lifelong foundation of parent/child trust. The only way you can "spoil" your child is to allow him/her to continue to behave like an infant long after he/she is psychologically capable of forgoing infantile behaviors.

Provide the Opportunity for Your Child To Develop a "Secure Attachment"

Current research has shown that one of the most important things parents can give their children during the first few years of life is the opportunity to develop a "secure attachment." A child who has a secure attachment is confident that his/her parents will be available, responsive, and helpful.

You can help your child develop a secure attachment by being readily available, sensitive to his/her different communications, and lovingly responsive when he/she seeks protection, comfort, and assistance. Whenever your infant cries, reach out to him/her and provide comfort. This nurturing response will enable your infant to continue to increase his/her self-confidence and feelings of security as well as enhance his/her exploratory activities and development of creativity. This assurance not only allows your child to boldly explore his/her world and encourages an ongoing sense of competence, but it will also help your child learn to regulate him/herself. Keep in mind that your child will model your behavior including treating him/herself in the same way you treat him/her.

The issue of self-regulation/self-management is extraordinarily important. Since your child will learn to do for him/herself what has been done for and to him/her, it is crucial that you provide consistent external regulation, reassurance, and support. Over a period of time your child will learn to reassure, calm, and regulate him/herself. Children who do not have consistent experiences of external regulation, reassurance, and support beginning in infancy and continuing throughout early childhood will develop an "anxious attachment." In addition to feeling almost constant anxiety, they will remain dependent on others, they will have low self-confidence in times of stress, and they will probably not trust others to provide any type of reassurance when they reach out to them.

Since children with anxious attachments feel uncertain about whether or not one or both of their parents will be available, responsive, or helpful, they tend to exhibit various forms of separation anxiety. They also tend to be hostile and often seek extensive attention. These anxious children may appear to be tense, impulsive, and easily frustrated, or they may seem passive and helpless until someone finally helps them. Some studies have shown that whiney, clingy, anxious children may also be ill tempered and prone to bully other children.

For better or for worse, the kind of attachment your child develops with you will tend to persist, remain unchanged, and be self-perpetuating. Throughout their lives secure children will tend to respond to potential failure with increased effort while anxious children will show signs of helplessness and defeatism unless corrective experiences in later relationships and/or psychotherapeutic intervention helps them to develop trust, self-confidence, and self-regulation/self-management.

Additional Benefits of a "Secure" Child

The positive, nurturing attention you give your child in the early days and years of his/her life will benefit you as well as him/her. The secure attachment your child develops with you will help make him/her happier and less demanding than children who develop anxious attachments. This not only makes parenting more rewarding but also more time/cost effective.

Investing a large amount of time and effort in being available, responsive, and helpful for your infant will pay high dividends over your lifelong relationship. On the other hand investing a small amount of time and energy in your infant may cost you tremendous amounts of time, energy, and possibly money later. Instead of enjoying the happiness that comes from an ongoing secure parent/child relationship, you may experience the frustration, anger, and heartache that comes with a troubled, anxious parent/child relationship.

In addition, investing all the time and energy it takes to provide a nurturing, responsive happy home environment for your infant will help you feel more confident as a parent and more attached to your child. Not only will you have a calm baby, but you will be helping your child learn the self-management and behavioral skills he/she needs to successfully engage in social relationships and face the challenges of the everyday world for the rest of his/her life.

Tips on Developing Better Parenting Behaviors

- Don't unquestioningly replicate your parent(s)' behaviors. Instead assess what your parent(s) did for and to you and then decide which techniques, perhaps some of your parent(s)' in combination with new ones described in this book and other sources of parenting information, will best meet your child's individual needs. Your goal is to give your child something better than your parents gave you.
- Avoid unconsciously replicating potentially harmful parenting

behaviors by becoming aware of your automatic responses. Monitor what you do for and to your child and look for behaviors that replicate your mother's or father's behaviors.

- Keep in mind that your natural tendency—especially if you feel stressed—will be to replicate what your parents did for and to you, but these behaviors will probably not have a positive impact on your child due to your differences in personality, temperament, and changing cultural nuances.

- Assess your own and your child's temperament and affect and then use parenting techniques that will help your child continue to grow and reach his/her full potential as an individual.

- Strive to provide a relaxed, supportive, positive home environment, which may be vastly different from what you experienced as a child.

- Take a positive rather than negative or judgmental attitude toward your child so that you will increase his/her self-esteem and self-confidence, two key components in your child's current as well as future successes.

- Whenever you feel excessively envious or resentful that your child "has it better" than you did as a child, stop and question both your response and your parenting behaviors.

- Continuously reaffirm your goal of developing and using parenting techniques that have a positive impact on your child.

- Remember that crying serves a purpose but it is not manipulative. Picking up your infant every time he/she cries will *not* spoil him/her—you can never show your child too much concern and affection!

- Responding consistently and reliably to your child's cries will help him/her to develop trust and faith in you and others who care for him/her, which leads to trust and faith in him/herself and the development of frustration tolerance and impulse control.

- For better or for worse, the kind of attachment your child develops with you will tend to persist, remain unchanged, and be self-perpetuating.

- Throughout their lives secure children will tend to respond to potential failure with increased effort while anxious children will show signs of helplessness and defeatism.

- Investing the time and energy it takes to provide a nurturing, responsive happy home environment for your infant will help you feel more confident as a parent and more attached to your child.

CHAPTER 4

MAINTAINING A POSITIVE, MUTUALLY SATISFYING RELATIONSHIP

Your relationship with your child will last the rest of your life, and to help ensure that relationship remains one of mutual love and respect, you must continuously nurture it. If you were buying a house or a car that you knew in advance would have to last you the rest of your life, you would probably be motivated to take extraordinary care of that house or car starting with the first day you got it. Since your relationship with your child is far more important and precious than any house or car, you should give your parent-child relationship even more extraordinary care starting with the very first day your child comes into your life—perhaps the day you learned you would become a parent—and continuing every day after.

Maintaining a positive, mutually satisfying parent-child relationship takes more than simply spending quality time with your son or daughter on an intermittent basis. It takes ongoing and consistent efforts to build trust with your child, providing appropriate structure, establishing appropriate rules, communicating clearly, dealing with conflicts in a sensitive way, serving as a positive role model, introducing a success-oriented work ethic, and teaching your child how to think in terms of options.

Continue To Build Trust, the Foundation of a Positive Relationship

You build trust with your child—or any other person, adult or child—by behaving in ways that are consistent, reliable, dependable, and predictable. Your child will experience you as a trustworthy person if you consistently respond to him or her in the same ways, always do what you say you will do, and continue to act consistently and reliably over a long period of time and in a wide range of situations. If you lovingly respond on a repeated basis whenever your infant cries, he/she will soon learn that you will be there to help in times of distress. If you feed your infant on a consistent basis, he/she will soon begin to realize that you will meet his/her needs.

Since infants and children are extraordinarily perceptive of their caregivers' underlying attitudes, take care to always respond to your child in a *loving* consistent, reliable, dependable manner. You have probably experienced someone giving you a gift and at the same time "spoiling" that gift with their reluctant, resentful, begrudging attitude, which can come from being envious of you, giving you something they don't really want to give at the time, or giving you something they don't believe you need. A gift as simple as the words "Great job!" can communicate either honest, sincere congratulations or cutting sarcasm depending on the giver's underlying attitude, true meaning, tone of voice, body language, and other verbal and nonverbal cues.

To avoid "spoiling" the care you give to your child, assess your attitudes and beliefs about your child and his/her needs, your role as one of his/her primary caregivers, and your capacity to respond lovingly when you are tired, sick, or under stress. Do whatever it takes to develop and maintain a genuine, consistent loving approach to your child and in meeting his/her daily needs. While you will not always be able to respond with exuberance, excitement, and absolute pleasure, you should strive to consistently respond in a positive way out of your underlying love and concern for your child.

Consistency does not simply mean being in the same place and doing the same thing at the same time every day. It also means *presenting yourself* in a consistent manner in terms of your attitudes and emotions. As your child experiences consistency and predictability in your behavior, attitudes, and emotions, he/she will develop a sense of confidence in you and your parent-child relationship. You can strengthen your child's confidence in you by consistently responding to conflict in a way that reduces that conflict rather than maintaining or heightening it. Consistent conflict reduction requires enormous effort on your part, but it will increase your personal sense of self-esteem and also give you pleasure in your own ability to function in a positive way on behalf of your child.

In addition, by continuing to build trust with your child by consistently responding to him or her in loving, predictable, conflict-reducing ways, you are modeling positive behaviors that he/she will later imitate. Keep in mind that your child will do as you do, not as you say. Your child will learn a lot about how to manage him/herself and how to manage relationships with others from his/her experiences with you.

Add Structure for Security

Most children *need* structure. Although some children can survive and even enjoy an unstructured situation, the majority thrive in a home that is relatively structured. Structure means that things happen at relatively predictable times during the course of each day and a predictable sequence of events will happen over the course of a day or week. By providing clear, consistent structure, you help your child learn to predict mealtimes, bedtimes, and other daily activities, which makes him or her feel more secure.

If both you and your spouse work or if you are a single parent, you probably have already established some structure simply to get the things done that need to be done at home. Be sure your structured time allows for daily individualized contact between each parent and each child. This will not only increase the quality of your parent-child relationship, but it will also serve to significantly increase your child's self-esteem. Your child needs to know that there is a predictable time each day when you will devote yourself to him/her. Your child also needs to feel that you believe he/she is worth devoting time to—that you value him/her enough to make spending time with him/her a top priority.

If for one reason or another you cannot physically be with your child every day, you can still provide a sense of consistency and predictability by communicating with him/her by writing letters or cards, sending E-mail, or calling on the telephone. Children sometimes have difficulty talking on the phone and are not always the best conversationalists, but all children feel excited—even thrilled—when they get mail addressed just to them. Your letters do not have to be lengthy, but you do need to send them on a consistent basis to let your child know that you are devoting part of each day to him/ her—*that* is the essential message.

Some parents, especially if their children are young, communicate by Skype, videophones, etc. so that their children can both hear and see them every day even when they are away from home. You can also record a book on audiotape so you can "read" to your child before he/she goes to sleep on nights when you can't be with him/ her.

Avoid giving your child expensive gifts as reminders of how much you love them. Although these may provide momentary pleasure and eventually become family heirlooms, the simpler things you do on a consistent basis will mean more to your child than anything else. Try leaving notes especially for your child on the table, in his/her lunchbox, or on his/her bed—or slip a piece of gum or favorite candy under his/her pillow. These little gifts will mean a lot. They let your child know that you love him/ her, you think he/she is worth spending time on, and your relationship with him/ her is important to you.

Establish Rules for Stability

Along with establishing a reliable structure for your child, also establish clearly defined rules—and *follow them consistently.* You and your child will do much better if you have five rules that both you and your spouse agree on and follow consistently than if you have fifty rules that come and go depending on your or your spouse's mood, the time of day, or some other extraneous factor. Applying rules inconsistently tends to frustrate and confuse children.

No matter how consistent you try to be however, you will undoubtedly have days when things go awry and the rules you have established will not be followed to the letter. That's perfectly acceptable. In fact you should be relatively flexible about the rules you establish, and you should also assess, and if necessary, modify your rules periodically as your child grows and matures or your family situation changes in other ways. For instance, a rule that served you and your child well when he/she was three years old probably will have little application when he/she turns nine. Continuing to follow unreasonable rules simply for the sake of consistency will create disharmony and conflict rather than security and stability.

Communicate Clearly—Both Consciously and Unconsciously

Whenever you communicate with your child, try to send him/ her a clear, simple, unambiguous message that clarifies whatever issues you are dealing with and is relatively consistent with what you have communicated in the past. What makes communicating clearly challenging is that we communicate both consciously and unconsciously.

Years ago Dr. Robert Langs and other researchers studied the differences between conscious and unconscious communication.[17] In conscious communication, which we use in everyday life to get work done, we send a single message that has no underlying innuendoes and does not require the receiver to have to guess about the intended meaning—we say what we mean and mean what we say. You need to use conscious, single-message communication with your child in order to help him/ her do what you need or want him/ her to do.

Avoid using unconscious communication with your child because he/she will have a very difficult time understanding exactly what it is you want him/ her to do. That's because in unconscious communication we say one thing but perhaps mean something else, and we send underlying innuendoes through carefully chosen words, facial expressions, gestures and other body language, sarcasm, and a variety of subtle verbal and nonverbal cues. Although some children are extraordinarily astute at reading their parents' unconscious communication and responding in such a way that completes this multi-level communicative system and others have learned from experience to question their parents if they are confused, most children take their parents at face value and respond only to the conscious message. This lack of clear communication usually leads to conflict, anger, disgust, and disappointment.

People tend to use a form of multilevel communication when they feel emotional distress, so learn to recognize when you are feeling stressed and take particular care at those times to communicate clearly. Always strive to send a single message to your child as simply as you can to minimize any chance of misunderstanding. *Before you begin communicating with your child, take a moment to clarify in your own mind exactly what message you need or want to send. Your goal always should be to give your child the information he/she needs to successfully achieve or accomplish a specific task or goal.*

Serve as a Positive Role Model

Once you become a parent, you begin living in the proverbial fishbowl. Your child will observe you with his/her eyes, ears, touch, smell, and every other way possible, and he/she will "record" everything you do and say over the next twenty years or so of your life. More importantly, your child will imitate you, and he/she will tend to do what you do, rather than what you say to do.

As a role model you help your child develop the skills he/she needs to become a successful, independent human being. In addition to modeling healthy impulse control, frustration tolerance, anticipation of consequences, conflict resolution, appropriate use of judgment, and a variety of other personal and social behaviors, you also model the values by which you live and presumably you want your child to adopt as his/her own. You cannot teach your child values simply by talking about them—you must also demonstrate adhering to those values in your everyday life. By your behavior you show your child how to enjoy social relationships, how to treat a spouse and other family members, how to entertain him/herself, how to balance

work and play, how to take care of his/her
body by eating healthy foods, participating
in physical activity on a regular basis, and
getting enough sleep, and all the other functions of daily living. Always take care to do
and be as you want your child to do and be.

Deal with Conflicts in a Sensitive Way

Children can benefit greatly from observing
how their parents resolve conflicts, but parents should take care to address major areas
of disagreement, financial concerns, marital
difficulties, and parenting issues in private,
outside their children's view and hearing.
Be sensitive to what conflicts may increase
your child's anxiety about his/her own security and/or relationship with one parent or
the other, and avoid discussing these issues
in front of your child.

Your child will have an especially hard time
dealing with issues that force him/her to side
with one parent because he/she has an attachment and loyalty to both parents. Putting
your child in a position of having to decide
and support one parent invariably makes him/

her feel disloyalty, guilt, and fear of loss of attachment to the other parent.

Introduce a Success-Oriented Work Ethic

Studies of resilient children,[18] those who lived in extremely difficult negative circumstances yet grew up to be successful adults, indicate that being responsible for doing daily chores contributes to the development of high self-esteem, especially in boys. The researchers referred to the work these children did at home as "forced helpfulness."[19] Each child had stated and/or unstated chores he/she was required to do without pay. Furthermore, the family's well-being—sometimes even survival—depended on the child responsibly handling these chores every day.

These children knew the importance of their work—in fact, they considered what they did for their family as important as their parents going to a job and earning a paycheck. The value they placed on the completion of their daily chores bolstered their sense of self-worth. Even though they received no money or other tangible reward and usually very little gratitude for completing their work, they gained an invaluable amount of self-esteem and self-discipline.

You can provide a similar opportunity to help your child develop a strong sense of self-worth and self-discipline. While you probably won't assign your child a chore that directly affects the existence of your family, care-fully choose a chore or chores that signifi-cantly contribute to the daily well-being of the family as a whole. It can be anything from helping you set the table to feeding the fam-ily pets or making sure the garbage is taken out. Also be careful not to tie these chores to a tangible reward or excessive expressions of gratitude—rather let the satisfaction of responsibly completing his/her daily work be your child's primary reward. The work your child does at home will help him/her to develop a positive work ethic that will lead to suc-cesses in many areas throughout his/her life.

Teach Your Child How To Entertain Options

Children need to learn how to develop and entertain a wide range of different options so that they will be able to successfully handle the myriad complex situations they will face every day of their life. You can teach your child about options whenever he/she does something you wish he/she hadn't.

Begin by asking your child why he/she did the objectionable act. Your child will probably answer, "I don't know." At this point most parents ask their children, "What should you have done instead?" Most children will again answer, "I don't know." Instead of wasting time, energy, and patience repeatedly attempting—probably without success—to get your child to come up with another "more appropriate" answer about what he/she will do in the future to avoid making the same mistake, take this opportunity to *teach* your child about options. Offer some suggestions, ask your child what he/she thinks, and practice those options.

Take every opportunity that arises to teach your child how to develop and entertain options. For instance, show your child different routes to the grocery store and then start letting him or her suggest which route to take. Do the same with changing a recipe, resolving a conflict, planning a family activity, and other situations that lend themselves to determining and making choices. By encouraging your child to take a flexible approach to tasks and other activities, you will be teaching him or her to think creatively and be adaptive, which in turn will help him or her successfully manage a wide range of situations without undue stress.

Tips on Maintaining a Positive, Mutually Satisfying Relationship

- You must continuously nurture your relationship with your child to ensure that it remains one of mutual love and respect.
- Continue to build trust with your child by behaving in ways that are consistent, reliable, dependable, and predictable.
- As much as possible make sure things happen at relatively predictable times during the course of each day and at a predictable sequence of events over the course of a day or week so that your child will have the predictable, reliable

environment he/she needs to feel secure.

- Establish clearly defined rules— and *follow them consistently* to increase your child's feelings of security and stability.

- Before you begin communicating with your child, clarify in your own mind exactly what message you need or want to send. Always strive to give your child the information he/ she needs to successfully achieve or accomplish a specific task or goal.

- Strive to always serve as a positive role model.

- Avoid putting your child in the anxious position of having to choose between you and his/her other parent by resolving major conflicts in private, outside your child's view and hearing to avoid causing him/her undue anxiety.

- Introduce your child to a success-oriented work ethic by giving him/ her the responsibility for at least one "important" daily chore.

- Teach your child how to think creatively and be adaptive by encouraging him/her to develop and entertain options in a wide variety of situations.

CHAPTER 5

USING DISCIPLINE TO HELP YOUR CHILD DEVELOP SELF-DISCIPLINE

Most people think that discipline only has to do with punishment—but discipline also relates to self-control. And while people generally react negatively to a child who "needs discipline," they admire a child who shows "self-discipline."

Beginning in infancy you can help your child develop self-discipline by gradually weaning him or her from external management while encouraging him/ her to develop internal management of a variety of behaviors including impulse control, frustration tolerance, anticipation of consequences, capacity to concentrate, and eventually concern for others as well as for him/herself. A child who has learned to control him/herself will not only receive admiration and praise, but he/ she will also enjoy an increased sense of self-esteem and self-confidence, positive traits that play key roles in success in a variety of situations.

Help Your Child Develop Internal Management

With your loving support and encouragement your child will gradually mature from being an infant dependent on you and others to manage his/her behaviors to a child with a growing capacity for internal management and eventually to a fully functioning individual with a high level of self-management. For instance, for the first year and a half or so of your child's life, you or another caregiver will change his/her diaper as needed. As your child approaches his/her second birthday however, you have begun potty training and you expect him/her to start developing self-management in this area. By the time he/she turns four, you will expect him/her to have developed the self-control to take primary responsibility for controlling his/her body and using the bathroom instead of wearing a diaper.

Your child develops self-control of his/her emotions in the same way. At first you will have to intervene to calm and soothe your child when he/she is either upset or overexcited, but you gradually intervene less and encourage him/her to take more responsibility for his/her own feelings. As your child matures you expect him/her to self-modulate his/her level of feelings and control the degree to which he/she responds in different situations without your intervention.

While some children learn to control their feelings relatively quickly, others take a longer period of time to develop this aspect of self-control. In general, by the age of three you should expect your child to take over more and more of the behavior management functions that you have been handling for him/ her. By this time your child should be able to soothe him/herself when upset and calm him/herself before he/she gets overly excited. Temper tantrums should diminish after age two, and by the time your child turns six, you should expect him/her to be able to appropriately manage feelings of anger and rage.

Model Self-Discipline

You also help your child develop self-discipline by modeling internal management behaviors. Like it or not you started living in a fishbowl the day your child was born, and your child will emulate and mimic your behavior including how you handle yourself in daily situations. You provide the model for how to manage impulses and frustrations, resolve conflicts, and express positive and negative feelings. Perhaps the biggest challenge you face as a parent is keeping yourself in check when it would be much easier—and perhaps more satisfying in the short term—to simply let go.

Your behavior will set the standard of acceptable and expected responses in your home, which places the burden on you to clearly demonstrate healthy self-discipline in all aspects of your own life. As your child emulates your behavior, he/she will begin to internalize your self-management techniques and gradually take more and more responsibility for his/her own behavior.

Give Your Child Nonverbal Cues To Help Them Regain Self-Control

As your child learns self-discipline, you may want to teach him/her nonverbal cues you can give from across a room, if need be, to remind him/her to control his/her behavior.

In some situations all a parent has to do is give a look, raise an eyebrow, or take a particular stance for their child to regain self-control and to maintain that control for a long period of time. The parent's look or raised eyebrow may not have even hinted at an accompanying punishment—the visual cue alone was enough to convey the parent's disappointment in the child, which in turn prompted the child to call him/herself into check.

Other children however are not as sensitive or attentive to their parents' facial expressions, moods, affects, or body language. This can cause extraordinary frustration if the parents themselves had been sensitive as children and now expect their own children to respond the same way they did. In these cases though, perhaps the child simply doesn't "see" or pick up on the parent's visual cues, or perhaps the child doesn't attend to the parent or for some reason isn't concerned about disappointing the parent. Work with your child to establish nonverbal cues that you can give and he/she will recognize as a message to calm down and behave in the expected, acceptable manner.

How To Deal with Strong-Willed Children

Children who consistently fail to behave in the manner their parents have taught and expect are often considered to be "difficult," to "need help," or to be "strong- willed." Unfortunately parents and other adults some-times tend to consider being strong -willed a negative trait when it can be a very positive trait that leads to success. A strong-willed person has the assertiveness to exact what he/she needs from the world as well as the internal support for the determination to complete tasks that are often begun in the face of frustration.

Like all other aspects of human behavior, strong will lies on a continuum that ranges from mild to excessive and can be either progressive or regressive. A child with a progressive strong will aims at succeeding in tasks and demonstrates a healthy deter-mination, stick-to-itiveness, autonomy, and a move toward independence. A strong-willed two or three-year-old, for instance, may insist on riding a tricycle—and later a bicy-cle—by him/herself and pushes his/her parent's hands away as he/she takes great pride in doing on his/her own. An extraordinarily healthy component of functioning allows a child to employ every asset he/she has at times to gain success in whatever endeavors he/she chooses. As a parent you need to continuously encourage healthy progressive strong will in your child so he/she can continue to succeed throughout life.

On the other hand children with regressive strong wills tend to refuse to participate in tasks. They seem to take an oppositional position rather than working toward autonomous functioning. As a parent you will have the most difficulty dealing with your child whenever he/she demonstrates regressive strong-willed behavior. Your challenge will be to help him/ her learn to use his/her assets in a positive way so that he/she develops a competent sense of mastery in tasks and a feeling of success.

Provide Unconditional, Loving Support

Studies indicate that the number one contributing factor to a person's success as an adult is an availability of someone he/she perceived as providing unconditional positive regard for him/her during childhood. Having a positive, supportive, long-term relationship with at least one person—who may not be either of the parents but often is—helps a child develop internal management as well as resiliency. Your child needs someone—you or another person—he/she can turn to, talk with, and express his/her misgivings about life or failures without fear of physical or emotional abandonment and/or any form of ridicule. Over time your child will develop absolute trust that this person has their best interest in mind and at heart.

This child-centered relationship is based on love rather than the need for the child to "look good" or behave in a way that pleases others. *This loving, supportive relationship provides the security your child needs as he/she practices and gradually masters the behavioral and socialization skills needed to progress from external to internal management and eventually to a high level of self-discipline and competent autonomous functioning.*

Provide Routine and Structure

In general, children do well in an environment that provides routine and structure. The routine and structure you provide at home will help calm your child and also give him/her a growing internal sense of regulatory capacities that allows him/her to make predictions about life that are fulfilled.

This does not mean that everything in your house and daily routine must be absolutely scheduled and organized. Rather it means that you have established a general consistency in the way things are done at home that allows your child to successfully anticipate activities, plan their day, and organize his/her life and thoughts.

You might want to start when your child is young by preparing him/her in advance for each day. You can simply sit down with him/her before bedtime and tell him/her what activities are planned for the next day. That information will resonate in your child's mind during the night, and he/she will awaken ready for the new day instead of wondering what will happen.

As your child gets older you can have a family meeting once a week to talk about special events or changes from your established normal routine. Family meetings offer a wonderful opportunity for you and your child to discuss, plan, and anticipate any changes in practical terms of what is needed to carry out the planned activities.

While older children—and some adults, depending on their personality—appear to like surprises, the majority of young children do not enjoy being surprised. Surprises tend to overstimulate them and shock their systems, usually resulting in a loss of self-control. You may want to hold off on surprising your children until they turn nine or even ten.

Establish Effective House Rules

Establishing a system of rules that apply to everyone in the house will provide a basic reliable structure that will help your child develop self-discipline. Start including your child in family discussions about house rules from an early age. Since the effectiveness of house rules depends on everyone in the house agreeing what the rules should be, limit the number of rules to those everyone accepts and that you as a parent are willing to enforce. It is far better to have three rules that everyone agrees on than ten rules that are important to one parent or other family member but not to others.

When you enforce the house rules, remember to "choose your battles carefully." As your child grows up you will inevitably engage in minor conflicts, small battles, and occasionally all-out war over a rule that he/she no longer agrees is reasonable. Remember that for any number of reasons, some children are so determined to please their parents that they will have no difficulty following a three-page list of rules on a daily basis. And for any number of different reasons, other children are not nearly so invested, which does not necessarily mean they love their parents any less than the totally obedient children—they simply are unable to abide by or get interested in following rules. Whenever you and your child disagree about the enforcement of a rule, step back from the situation and ask yourself how important that specific issue is in the overall picture of your child's development and the family's functioning. Depending on how much, if anything, the issue really counts, you may want to modify or even drop the rule—but only after you have a family discussion about it.

Family discussions about rules help your child learn a variety of invaluable lessons about life. First he/she will learn the importance of different issues in life. Next he/she will begin to understand that most issues are neither black nor white—they are some shade of gray. He/she will then discover that everything has gradients, levels of importance or intensity. For instance, he/she will learn that some issues are far more important than others and that some issues make people feel more angry than other issues.

To help your child understand the concept of gradients, you can rate issues, family rules, and experiences on a scale of 1 to 10, with unimportant issues that have very little if any impact on anybody at the 1 end of the scale and life and death issues at the 10 end. Realistically very few issues, rules, or experiences reach the importance of a 10, but people sometimes tend to either blow a relatively unimportant issue out of proportion by making it a 10 or blow off a very important issue by making it a 1. Work with your child to help him/her learn to properly assess an issue, rule, or experience and place it in the appropriate place on the continuum of 1 to 10.

You may want to turn this learning experience into a game by describing a variety of issues, rules, or experiences and having your child place them on the 1 to 10 continuum. Every time your child comes within one point of what you perceive the appropriate value to be, you give him/her a point, and when he/she accumulates a previously agreed on number of points, you give him/her an appropriate reward.

Develop an Effective Discipline Program

You have many discipline techniques to choose from to use at home to help your child develop self-control. As in everything else you do for and with your child, you need to tailor your discipline program to your child's personality and abilities as well as the unique qualities of your parent-child relationship. Techniques that work well with one child or in one parent-child relationship may not work at all with others.

You will find information on different types of behavioral and/or discipline techniques readily available in books, magazines, videos, and other materials. In addition, members of your family as well as friends, caregivers, and other adults will quite often spontaneously share with you how they "trained" their children to behave. In fact, you will have more than enough ideas—your challenge will be to combine specific techniques in a discipline program that builds on your child's growing sense of competence and helps him/ her to achieve internal mastery of his/her behavior.

Rather than review and explore every available technique, I offer you the following range of general guidelines and recommendations that you can use to design a program that will work well for you and your child. Be sure to incorporate techniques that will contribute to your child's growing sense of self-confidence and long-term—rather than just immediate—competence as a self-disciplined individual. Although occasionally it may be necessary for you to immediately stop your child from acting in a particular way simply because it is bothersome or perhaps even dangerous, the focus of your discipline program should be to help your child attain long-term competence in self-control as well as a sense of internal mastery of his/her behavior.

Plan a Program that Progressively Achieves the Desired Results

Plan a program that takes your child from A to B to C and eventually to Z rather than from A to Z all at once. For instance, if you want your child to gain self-control over a behavior that you consider to be inappropriate, don't expect to use a single discipline technique that will eliminate the behavior in one day—rather use one or more techniques that will gradually reduce the behavior over a period of time until it is eliminated. Remember that everyone, children as well as adults - your child as well as you - has a hard time changing their behavior, so plan a step-by-step program to make it as easy as possible for your child to successfully master self-control in each new situation.

Use Punishment Appropriately

Recent research has shown that any discipline/behavior management program that is based entirely on punishment is doomed to fail—both in the short and long term.

Research has also shown that children as well as adults tend to work much harder to earn a reward than to avoid punishment. In one older study, for instance, some factory workers were offered a reward if they produced more "widgets" while other workers were threatened with docking of pay, loss of overtime hours, and/or loss of position if they did not meet certain quotas. In this and similar studies the workers who were offered a reward—a positive intervention—generally produced more "widgets" than the workers who were threatened with some type of punishment—a negative intervention.

In another older study, a group of workers was offered a reward for turning out quality work for the "good of the company" while a second group was threatened with punishment if quality did not improve. Again, the workers who were given the positive intervention performed better. They tended to turn out high-quality products while the workers who were given the negative intervention tended to produce flawed ones, something that would have cost the company in the long run.

From studies like these as well as personal experience, managers in industrial companies have learned to provide positive incentives and interventions to motivate their workers to produce high-quality products. Studies on children have shown the same principle: To achieve long-term positive results use rewards instead of punishment to shape behavior.

If for some reason you must occasionally use a punishment to immediately stop a destructive or annoying behavior, make it a short-term punishment. For instance, if you are planning to take away a privilege or toy, make it for only one day at a time, especially if your child is young. That way your child will be able to wake up each morning and start fresh rather than having a punishment hanging over him/her. You may even want to make it for just a morning or afternoon so your child has an extra chance to start fresh after half a day.

Also remember that whenever your child breaks a rule or misbehaves, reprimand and if necessary punish him/her appropriately and make that the end of the interaction. Avoid seeking signs and/or behavior from your child

that express regret, sadness, and/or embarrassment—and more importantly avoid increas-
ing the punishment until your child does
show regret, sadness, or embarrassment. Many
children—like many adults—stoically suffer
the consequences of their behavior and then
get on with their activities without wanting
to deal any further with their "failure."
So if your child takes his/her punishment
appropriately and says the right words, don't
insist on or try to extract what you consider
to be the accompanying "proper attitude."

Most discipline programs work well on a day-
to-day basis, which means that as long as
your child shows self-control and behaves in
the expected manner according to the agreed
upon house rules, he/she should be allowed
to enjoy all of the appropriate privileges.
Whenever your child misbehaves, he/she loses
his/her privileges for the remainder of that
day—and perhaps may have to go to bed early
that night.

You can also combine a day-to-day program
with one of the various time-out techniques.
Whichever techniques you choose to use to
help your child develop self-discipline,
remember that *your child will tend to work*

harder to gain a reward than to avoid a punishment.

Use Appropriate Rewards

Using "rewards" does not mean investing in high-priced or even low-priced toys to give to your child whenever he/she demonstrates self-discipline. While you may find it helpful to use materialistic objects at particular times to encourage your child to achieve a particular behavior, using other kinds of rewards will help you strengthen your parent-child relationship.

These nonmaterialistic rewards include spending special time with your child on a one-to-one basis. If you are a working parent or have more than one child, each child will treasure the possibility of having you all to him/herself for a while. Depending on the behavior you expect your child to achieve, you could offer an entire day alone with you, a special breakfast, lunch or dinner at a special place, a walk through the woods, or even an additional fifteen to thirty minutes at the end of the day to spend reading a book, playing a game, or just cuddling. Offering your child the special reward to spend extra time with you will motivate him/her to work very hard to develop a growing sense of internal control over a wide range of feelings and behaviors.

Remember though that *your child should not have to earn all the time he/she spends alone with you*—you are offering *additional* time as a reward as part of your program to help your child develop self-discipline.

Design a Balanced System of Positive and Negative Interventions

The most effective discipline programs include a balance of rewards that can be earned and some things to avoid. For example, you could offer your child twenty minutes of special time with you at the end of the day if he/she achieves self-control over a particular behavior. If your child does not achieve that self-control then he/she goes to bed at the regular time, and if your child not only doesn't achieve that self-control but also regresses to a previous level of functioning then he/she goes to bed twenty minutes earlier than the regular time. This system allows your child to enrich his/her life by mastering an achievable goal, and it also provides reasonable consequences for not working toward an achievable goal.

You can also use a balanced approach with material rewards. If you reward your child with a particular item for mastering a certain behavior, give the item with the understanding that your child can keep the item as long as he/she maintains self-control over that behavior. So if your child earns the item one day and the following day regresses, he/she must return the item to you. You could add an additional consequence of regressing by agreeing ahead of time with your child that if he/she does not earn back the item within a set amount of time, then you may give the item to someone else—perhaps a charitable cause—of *your* choosing, not your child's.

Include Appropriate Natural Consequences

Natural consequences involve the idea that whenever a child is involved in a behavior that is less than desirable there may be some type of naturally occurring result. For instance, if your child refuses to put on a

coat, you may decide to let him/her go outside without it simply to find out for him/
herself how it feels to be cold. Or if you
ask your child to bring in a ball he/she left
in the yard but he/she doesn't do it, someone
else may come along and take it.

Oftentimes natural consequences provide relatively quick, easy, powerful instructive experiences, but sometimes they provide negative
experiences that you cannot accept for one
reason or another. You must decide for yourself when suffering the natural consequences
of a particular behavior will best help your
child learn to control that behavior.

Do Not Spank!

Opinions about spanking have changed dramatically over the past fifty years in our
culture. As Eric Erickson, the famous anthro-
pologist, child analyst, researcher, and
lecturer noted, there are a wide number and
variety of cultures throughout the world and
each culture appears to raise children in a
manner that may differ significantly from other
cultures. Within each culture however, most
children grow up to be healthy and accepted

as part of that society, which provides ongoing support for that society's accepted discipline and child-management practices.

From a historical perspective spanking used to be a widely accepted means of child punishment in the United States, and until the 1970s many public schools continued to employ corporal punishment in some form. The schools received public support for spanking as well as other corporal punishments, and our culture also supported these forms of punishment at home—unless the corporal punishing went beyond what the particular subculture of a community considered acceptable.

In most cases no one questioned corporal punishment or expressed concern for the punished child, and children knew that if they misbehaved they might very well receive a spanking or worse. Quite often a child who failed to behave in the expected way was sent to his/her room to await either the spanking or being called to the specific room in the house where spankings generally took place with a specific somewhat formal ceremony. Before administering the punishment, the parent often told the child how much he/she regretted having to do the spanking and further discussed the lack of self-discipline that merited the spanking.

Beginning in the 1970s our culture began to reject spanking or other corporal punishment as acceptable disciplinary techniques. Today public schools no longer allow corporal punishment as the primary means of discipline, and most subcultures no longer accept spanking at home. With today's lack of cultural support for corporal punishment, children now experience spanking as abusive and consider it to be something that should not happen to them. In addition, parents who spank their children no longer feel societal support for this form of disciplinary action. Usually when a parent spanks a child today it is not the planned, expected, accepted punishment it used to be. Rather, spanking today tends to be an impulsive act on the part of a frustrated parent who feels that this is the only way to stop the undesirable behavior. Parents no longer talk about spanking with the former sense of prestige their own parents did—in fact, parents who spank their children now may feel guilty and/or ashamed at their own behavior in the situation.

In addition, some research studies have shown that spanking did not achieve the desired results—in fact children who were spanked at an early age continued the same or similar behaviors for which they continued to receive spankings. Other studies have shown that children who are spanked may stop the behavior but only in a public manner—they become "sneaky" and devious in carrying out similar behaviors behind their parents' backs. Parents sometimes have reported that children have requested a spanking, probably as a self-serving easy way out of a situation—despite the pain, a whack on the butt is quicker and easier to deal with than being grounded or losing privileges for a period of time.

The bottom line is *do not spank.* Spanking doesn't appear to be effective in stopping undesirable behaviors, our culture no longer accepts spanking as an expected disciplinary technique, and parents who spank their children may feel societal disrespect. In addition, many schools today teach children early on about a wide range of social and moral issues that include physical abuse. So most children know that spanking is not acceptable, and they consider parents who spank to be doing the wrong thing from a cultural as well as a legal point of view.

Incorporate Hobbies, Team Sports, and Other Success-Oriented Activities

Research studies on children who demonstrate resiliency, self-discipline, and competence as autonomous individuals have shown that hobbies, team sports, and other structured activities contribute to the development of self-discipline. You can start incorporating these kinds of success-oriented activities at home by involving your child in doing chores at home as soon as he/she is able to participate, even at a very minimal level. This will help to make your child feel that he/she is an integral part of the family functioning. As your child matures, involve him/her in church or other social activities outside the home as well as in school and sports activities. Your child's active involvement in healthy activities will help him /her develop his/her own identity as an individual, allow him/her to interact with children who are functioning well, and provide a range of adult role models who are functioning in a healthy way.

Tips on Using Discipline To Help Your Child Develop Self-Discipline

- Discipline relates to self-control as well as to appropriate punishment.
- Help your child develop self-discipline by gradually weaning him/her from external management while encouraging him/her to develop internal management of impulse control, frustration tolerance, anticipation of consequences, capacity to concentrate, and other behaviors.
- Model healthy self-discipline for your child in all aspects of your life.
- Teach your child nonverbal cues you can give from across a room, if need be, to remind him/her to exercise self-control.
- Continuously encourage healthy, progressive, strong will in your child so that he/she can continue to succeed throughout life.

- If your child demonstrates regressive strong will, do everything you can to help him/her channel his/her energy and efforts in a positive rather than negative direction.
- Strive to always give your child unconditional love and support.
- Provide a home environment that has routine and structure.
- Avoid big surprises until your child is nine or ten years old.
- Establish rules that everyone in your house—including your young child—understand and enforce the rules in a rational, responsible way.
- Teach your child about gradients in issues, rules, experiences, emotions, and other areas of life.
- Design an effective program that will help your child develop self-discipline. Incorporate behavior-management techniques that progressively achieve your desired results and include appropriate

rewards and punishments, a balance of positive and negative interventions, appropriate natural consequences, and hobbies, team sports, and other success-oriented activities.

- Do not spank your child!

CHAPTER 6

SOME NOTES ON DIVORCE

Although no one plans on a divorce when they marry and typically no one is planning on a divorce when they have their first child, the fact is that a larger and larger percentage of couples do in fact get divorced. Having conducted numerous child custody evaluations and sat in family court and observed what takes place, the following suggestions are offered for those who have to face this reality and wish to manage it in a manner that is least destructive for their children.

First, avoid at all costs creating situations in which your child or children are allowed to consider that it is their fault that their parents are divorcing.

Second, do not ever place a child in the position of feeling like they have to choose which parent they will live with. Simply put, it is not their choice. If parents can not agree on residential custody of the child, the court will.

Third, do not make a child the messenger because parents are unable to communicate directly. Equally, do not ever disrespect or speak badly about the other parent in front of the child (if you want the child to respect you).

Fourth, arrangements for child custody include everything from children spending equal time with each parent to extremely protected arrangements such as a parent only being allowed supervised visitation. Some parents live within blocks of each other and the child/children can go between their homes at will, while other parents live states (even countries) apart and creative arrangements are made.

The most important thing for parents to clearly understand is that: As the amount of open conflict and hostility between parents increases, the risk of emotional disturbance, poor school performance and poor relationship functioning both now, and in the future, increases significantly for their children.

Thus, while a divorce may be an unexpected, disappointing and painful reality, how you manage yourself and your ongoing relationship with "the other parent" will have a dramatic impact on your child/children.

END NOTES

Chapter 1: Building a Positive Relationship with your Infant or Toddler

1. C. Zeanah and M. Barton, ed, Special Issue, "Internal Representations and Parent-Infant Relationships," *Infant Mental Health Journal, Vol. 10, No. 3, Fall 1989.*

2. D. Stern, *Diary of a Baby* (New York: Basic Books, 1990).

3. T. Field, S.M. Schanberg, F. Scafidi, C.R. Bauer, N. Vega-Lahr, R. Garcia, J. Nystrom, and C.M. Kuhn, "Tactile/Kinesthetic Stimulation Effects on Preterm Neonates", *Pediatrics,* 77 (5), pp/654-8.

4. M. Mahler, F. Pine and A. Bergman, *The Psychological Birth of the Human Infant,* (New York: Basic Books, 1975), pp. 41-2.

5. C. Brenner, *An Elementary Textbook of Psychoanalysis,* (Garden City, NY: Revised Anchor Book, 1974).

6. D. Stern, *The Interpersonal World of the Infant,* (New York: Basic Books, 1985) pp. 39-42.

7. Ibid.

8. Ibid.

9. D.W. Winnicott, *The Maturational Processes and and Facilitating Environment,* (Madison, Conn.: International Universities Press, 1965), pp 145-52.

10. S.H. Fraiberg, E. Adeson, and V. Shapiro, "Ghosts in the Nursery: A Psychoanalytic Approach to the Problem of Impaired Infant-Mother Relationships," *Journal of American Academy of Child Psychiatry,* 1975, pp. 387-422.

11. N. Stern-Bruschweiler and D. Stern, "A Model for Conceptualizing the Role of the Mother's Representational World in Various Mother-Infant Therapies," *Infant Mental Health Journal,* Vol. 1, No. 3, pp 142-56.

12. D. Stern, Cape Cod Lecture, Summer, 1991.

13. C. Zeanah and M.Barton in "Internal Representations and Parent-Infant

Relationships, *"Infant Mental Health Journal,* Vol. 10, No. 3, Fall 1989.

14. B. Cramer, "Are Postpartum Depressions a Mother-Infant Relationship Disorder?" *Infant Mental Health Journal,* Vol. 14, No. 4, Winter 1993, pp. 283-7.

15. P. Lewis, The Five Key Habits of Smart Dads (Grand Rapids, MI: Zondervan Publishing House, 1994).

16. G. Russel and M. Rudojevic, "The Changing Roles of Fathers? Current Understandings and Future Directions for Research and Practice", Infant Mental Health Journal, Vol. 13, No. 4, Winter 1992, pp.296-311.

17. Pruett, K. Interviewed by Adler; Special Edition Newsweek; Spring/Summer 1977, Page 73.

Chapter 3: Developing Better Parenting Behaviors

1. Klein, M.; Envy and Gratitude & Other Works; 1946-1963; Delta, 1975, Pp 176-235.

Chapter 4: Maintaining a Positive Relationship

1. Langs, Robert; The Technique of Psychoanalytical Psychotherapy; (Jason Aronson, Inc., New York, 1973).

2. Byron, E.; Carlson, E. and Sroufe, A.; Resilience Process; Development and Psychopathology; Vol. 5; Fall 1993; #4, pp. 517-528.

3. Staudinger, U; Marsiske, M. and Baltes, P.; Resilience and Levels of Reserve Capacity in Later Adulthood: Perspectives from Life-Span Theory; Development and Psychopathology; Vol. 5, Fall, 1993, #4, pp. 541-566.

Made in the USA
Charleston, SC
01 May 2011